Sparks in the
Archive

Didi Bouchard-Gehorsam

Edited by Edie Zerazion

Book Cover by Elena Moore

Illustrations by Elena Moore

Advised by: Jean Bouchard, Catherine Saar, Bert Gehorsam, Lauren McHugh, Isaac Toledano, Hexy Rodriguez

First edition 2023

Sparks in the
Archive

I was always content with the silence, the nothingness. It was all I had ever known and I sat there patiently the whole time. I would have been happy to continue, but as it turned out, that wasn't my purpose.

A crash—the first noise I would ever hear—sounded through my thoughts and the emptiness around me, I thought that it might've ruptured my eardrums. It was quickly followed by a rush of colors I knew and often thought of, but I could never have imagined that they might be so beautiful.

The rest of my senses followed in quick succession, almost overstimulating but ultimately entrancing. The hues of reds and blues and colors for which I didn't have the names danced around my consciousness, accompanied by sounds of birds chirping at what must be dawn and the building scent of old wood.

Shapes began to take form, shelves upon empty shelves, how far I didn't know but could somehow feel. I felt ecstatic as they rose higher and spread farther, my purpose finally clicking in my mind.

I didn't even allow the shelves to finish placing themselves before they were filling, my pen moving across paper carrying words and stories that had filled my consciousness since it began, writing at a pace I couldn't quite quantify. I began hundreds of books all at once, working on them simultaneously, not wanting to forget even one sentence I had created. The pages flew and the shelves filled, and I wanted to smile as I watched my works take shape.

Though I worked fast, I put the utmost care, love, and thought into my stories, wanting to create the most wonderful paths for my characters as they made their choices and lived their lives. At the same time, my work was teaching me things about my own consciousness that I had never realized even in all my time alone, things I had never bothered to think of. I realized very quickly that I was meant to be a caretaker, and I felt no burden upon coming to that conclusion, only gratitude.

I don't know how long it took to fill the shelves, but I wrote until they were packed full, so quickly that not even dust could begin to settle on the spine of my very first book. An endless sea of series after series, stacked upon equally endless shelves. I looked around me, taking in the stunning sight and the crisp scent of new books. This was my space of my creation with my stories, and I quickly remembered the long-engrained feeling of contentedness; this time, though, I'd never be alone again.

That couldn't have been more true. As I contemplated my future, forever surrounded by the characters and stories I loved so dearly, I didn't notice the arrival of a new presence between my shelves. This entity walked the rows, skimming his fingers over the bindings of a particularly long and adventurous story I had written, before he stopped, one finger resting over the Roman numeral 'I' to mark the beginning of the series.

I didn't notice him until he walked around the corner, taking leisurely steps with his eyes flying through the paragraphs on the page. I was immediately overtaken by curiosity. Who was he, and moreover, what did he think of my book? I went to boldly introduce myself but discovered that I could not find my voice, and I instead watched the man continue to flip the pages.

"Another bore," said the librarian as he placed the final book onto the pile he had been working through as of late. The story he had just finished had felt far too similar to all the others he had been reading for so long, and he couldn't remember the last time he felt a real connection to any character in any story. This one was especially boring and repetitive, he felt, as it ended with a couple dying in each other's arms after decades of happy marriage. There was no adultery, painful trauma, or anything of the sort to add any stakes to the plot.

You could call him apathetic, but from an objective eye, he really was just bored. When one has nothing to do but dust shelves and reorganize books that no one will ever check out nor read, it's only reasonable that he'd yearn for an ounce of excitement, some change.

Those qualities were, of course, contained somewhere in these shelves, but the librarian seemed to have gotten himself lost amongst the endless sea of rom-coms and slow-burns, none of it interesting anymore.

I hated to watch him like this. It had always been the two of us alone, and he was much less fun when feeling exasperated and bored. He almost never acknowledged me in the first place, and was even more distant when he was agitated. I did my best to help him when he was in these moods, frankly because I didn't like being ignored. I needed enrichment just like anyone else, but I wasn't sure how to get him out of the shelves he was stuck between.

I knew him well, I thought, better than any character in any book he had ever read. I remembered watching him walk between this expanse of shelves for the first time, the excitement he felt for my stories shining in the brightness in his eyes. He once carried all that positivity and more as he walked the aisles and happily worked with me. He cared for me and my stories, keeping me going, and I provided him with entertainment to pass the endless time. We were both happy to have company.

***

I remembered silently watching him read for a long time, maybe days, his eyes never finding me. I wondered if he, too, could not speak, or if he chose not to because he thought he was alone. Either way, I found myself feeling thankful for the company. Watching his expressions as he took in my compositions was a new stimulation, something I had certainly never experienced in the true nothingness of my past.

I watched a single tear drop down his cheek as he finished that first series, and a second fell as he looked up, splashing down onto the final paragraph and barely disturbing the ink. I watched his face contort through a range of different emotions, studying the nuances, and beginning to understand their meanings.

***

But that shine was now replaced with a dull film, his feelings having shifted and diluted. We were both bored. He, because he had almost given up on finding a worthwhile story, and I, because I couldn't stand to watch him sulk. I knew I needed to do something, make a move to lure him to the outskirts of the genres he had been stuck in for so long.

I skimmed over the bindings on the shelves a little further down and found a story I loved, a coming of age. In this story, in an early year in the human timeline, a father and his young boy hunt by bow. The boy shoots well, and he—well I don't want to spoil the plot, that's no fun. Manners damned, I grabbed the book and flung it into the aisle where he could see.

"I'm not in the mood to play," he said plainly. I wanted to groan, always tired of how repetitive and bland he got when he was uninspired. He was silent beyond that, and I was immediately annoyed at having been ignored. He knew very well that I was just as alone as he, and it drove me insane that he would act as if I didn't exist just because he was in a mood. And unfortunately for him, on this specific day, *I* was not in the mood to put up with *his* attitude. I grabbed the next volume of my chosen story and flung it down the aisle, hitting him square in the back of the head.

He yelped, jumping straight up out of the armchair he had slouched himself into. He whipped his head around to the direction I had thrown from, looking ready to light me ablaze. Success! I thought, seeing that I had finally given him the activation energy for expression. Any feeling other than boredom was an improvement, regardless of the fact that the feeling was frustration. He looked down at his feet and toyed with the idea of picking up the book, but seemed to decide otherwise out of pure spite. He kicked it away and shivered when he felt my chill of annoyance that followed.

"You know it hurts when you throw that hard," he started to lecture, "you could give me a concuss–" I stopped him mid-thought by whacking him hard in the stomach with the third volume of the series, sending him to his knees, gasping for breath. I almost felt bad for that one, realizing I threw it a lot harder than I initially meant to, but I held back my empathy, reminding myself that the pain he felt was merely an illusion to the both of us. That thought wasn't especially comforting, knowing that the ephemeral sense of touch could feel so real, and I was thankful that I rarely had to put up with such a feeling.

The librarian regained his composure, straightened his back, and took a deep breath before speaking to me again.

"I'm getting sick and tired of you..." he mumbled, before bending over and picking up the volume that had just knocked his ego down a peg. He briefly read the back cover and looked around for where I had thrown the first volume. Defeated, he gave in to my suggestions, as he always did.

He sat back down in his armchair after finding the first volume, wishing he had a coffee but too tired to get one. Although I was pushy, I did empathize with him, so I quickly brought one and gently set it down, dark roast with sugar but no cream, on the table in front of him. He looked up from reading the back cover and I thought I saw a slight smile cross his features, but he wiped it away as fast as it had appeared, never wanting to give me the satisfaction through his frustration. He didn't thank me, but I felt his gratitude anyway, and I found myself reminiscing again.

***

He began to round each corner with intention, like he was looking for something, and just as I had convinced myself that he couldn't, he spoke. It was soft, mostly whispered to himself, and nothing more complex than the want for a coffee.

I jumped to action, wanting to make some sort of a connection with him, and quickly placed one on the small table at the end of the aisle he walked through. He stopped in his tracks as his eyes landed on the small white mug, steam lightly billowing into the dim light cast by the dawn.

He stared for a few moments, and I could see the gears turning in his head through his raised eyebrow and partially panicked eyes. He crept towards the small table, suddenly much more aware of his surroundings than he had been mere moments before.

He glanced into the dark liquid in the cup, the steam already dissipating as he caught a glimpse of his reflection, his features showing his apprehension to touch the mug. But he finally did, at first just lightly touching the ceramic to discover that it was in fact hot, and then timidly picking it up and taking a small sip.

***

I brought myself back to the current reality as he begrudgingly opened the book to its first page. Annoyance crossed his face after finding that there was no summary on the back cover, only a short biography of the main character. I don't know what he expected, that's how I always presented my books. A summary would ruin the surprise. He took a sip of the coffee—perfect, as always—before reading the first words of the book I had offered to him.

***

Alexander woke from a deep sleep, cold again. He had rolled too far onto his side in the night, accidentally falling out from underneath the pelt he shared with his father. He quickly rolled back to his original warm position, hoping to shake the chill out of his bones.

"You're awake, Boy?" his father asked, sounding alert.

"Yes, Father, but barely," he groaned, having a hard time blinking the sleep from his eyes. Alexander always had difficulty waking when he was cold. His father slowly rose from his position on the cot, deeply breathing in the chilled morning air. He looked around longingly, distracted by a wave of nostalgia as he took in the almost empty cottage.

Alexander looked at his father, who seemed to be caught in a daze of memory. Alexander knew his father often thought of his late wife, Alexander's mother, whose presence alone washed the cottage in a warm glow. The wrinkles on his face showed his waning strength, a sad side effect of the sickness that riddled him. Alexander knew he wished for nothing but to provide for his family, and that he regretted that he could not. Now he was weak, almost frail, hunched in stature and looking on the verge of a break.

Alexander felt his father's longing and looked at the sad expression on his face. He reminded himself that, although he was young, he had a new responsibility to take on after his mother's departure from the mortal plane. He had become the provider.

He missed the herbs and vegetables his mother would return with after her days of foraging, wishing he had the chance to learn from her. He was tired of eating flavorless meats day after day, but was afraid to poison his father or himself by picking the wrong herb. He wished again that he had a sister who might have learned his mother's gift for nature.

Alexander glanced at the stock of cured meat his father and he kept, knowing already that he'd be disappointed by what he saw. As expected, the stock was extremely low, and what was still there was on the verge of going bad. They had to hunt, and they had to do it today.

Alexander rose as his father sat solemnly, a familiar sight. He thought longingly back to when he wasn't burdened with such responsibility, but he shook the notion from his mind. His father didn't wish to get sick, and his mother didn't wish so either, so there was no purpose in Alexander's life for resentment. He was tired, but he was strong and healthy, and he had learned well from his father in the previous years. He picked up his bow and slung it over his back, attaching his quiver to his waist.

"Are you going to come along Father? We need to start now if we want to catch anything," Alexander stated, knowing it as fact. The father smiled, proud of his boy for how he had picked up so easily on hunting tactics, knowing everything like the back of his hand.

Dawn was about to break, and though the creatures they hunted could see better than the men in the dark, they were always tired and sluggish as they rose from their slumber. His father finally made the effort to rise from the cot, stretching his aching limbs as he did so. His joints creaked and his bones burned, but he ignored it for the sake of his son. He didn't want him to know how much pain he was in daily, not wanting to concern Alexander with the possibility of losing the rest of his remaining family.

Alexander took his father's hand, helping him maintain his balance as he stretched. His father did not take long to prepare for their journey, only putting on the shoes his wife had crafted so long ago and slinging his larger bow and his quiver over his back. Though his son did most of the hunting at that point, he liked to be prepared for the rare occasion that a tired or injured deer would move slowly enough for him to draw the bowstring and take his shot.

***

The librarian groaned and smacked his head down onto the pages, before lifting it and stating, "This is going too slow, are they ever going to do any hunting?"

I felt annoyed; the librarian had a bad habit of doing this, disregarding the importance of exposition and losing patience over just a few pages. He had no idea of how interesting the small stories could be, he now saw them as nothing but trivial.

I saw this snap occur in him a mere couple of months prior, or maybe that's just when I took notice of it. For so long, he had enjoyed the stories I wrote, connected with the characters, and expressed a range of emotions that I rarely saw anymore. I wondered how long it had been since the change began, when he started forgetting to care. At this point, I didn't even know what he was interested in anymore. But all I could do was keep him reading. After all, there was nothing else to do, and, selfishly, I deeply needed the enrichment, regardless of his reactions.

I flipped the page for him, trying to keep his attention on the story before him. He groaned and I wanted to hit him on the back of the head again, but refrained. Something in me said that he would not be very responsive to force anymore, and I reminded myself that he was already frustrated with me from earlier. I didn't very much want him to withdraw from the stories I presented to him, hoping that he retained any curiosity at all.

Clearly still annoyed but sensing my urgency, he read on.

***

The woods were still, dew hanging onto the leaves and blades of grass, shining in the early morning light. His father followed a few paces behind Alexander, not wanting him to see the limp he had been developing those past weeks. He felt, this morning in particular, that he was fighting to wake up, overwhelmed with clouded thoughts that he may be waking in the afterlife. This thought was quickly knocked out of him as he stepped on a rock the wrong way, feeling it stab him through his well-worn shoes. He took a deep breath, oddly reveling in the pain he felt, as it was a reminder that he did, in fact, wake up that morning, and that he had not left his son. Not yet.

Alexander suddenly stopped in his tracks, putting out his arm to signal to his father to do the same. He cocked his head to the side, hoping to hear another crunch of a branch like the one he thought he just heard. Silence; not even the breath of the wind could be heard. That was perfect though, any noise would cut through that in an instant.

And then there it was, the crunch of leaves under a hoof. Perfect. They had eaten nothing but rabbit and squirrel for weeks, a deer or boar would significantly improve their lives for weeks. Perhaps it was good fortune, a sign that there may be success for future hunts. Alexander looked to where he heard the sound and was astounded at the size of the deer his eyes were met with. A large doe, not miraculous or irregular in size, but larger than he had seen in a long time. He was worried and questioned his actions for a moment, afraid to discard any of the meat from the deer, not wanting to waste even an ounce of her sacrifice.

But he reminded himself of his role and took the next step anyway, silently drawing an arrow from his waist and taking aim. His moves were, in the end, decisive and quick, as he shot with perfect aim and killed her with only one arrow. 'Thank you,' he thought, feeling great gratitude for the fact that she didn't suffer.

"Well done, Boy," his father said, astounded at how far his son's accuracy had improved since he started teaching him to hunt, merely two years earlier. He was growing into a fine young man, and his father was extremely proud. He hated the thought, but he was thankful to feel assured that his son would be perfectly fine when he passed on, and he felt that the time was drawing nearer with every passing sunrise.

Alexander smiled briefly, thankful for his father's approval—

***

The librarian groaned yet again,

"This boy lives the dullest life. If I had to fight or hunt just for my dad to be proud, I'd move on from him. There are so many easier ways to gain satisfaction."

This viewpoint made me frustrated, alarmed even. The librarian showed no care for the father's pain and the effort he put into his survival for the sake of his son. The librarian seemed to value self-satisfaction over community and gratitude, a stance that appeared to be growing in him lately.

I felt exhausted, as this story was close to my heart, though I could say that about all of my stories. This was a story of family and perseverance, joy and loss, passion and romance and fire and so on. He didn't even give it a chance to pick up before being so quick to judge its pace and purpose.

The librarian next did something that annoyed me beyond belief: he went back to the shelf and picked the eleventh volume of the same story, and flipped right to the end.

***

Alexander smiled at Cassandra softly as she held him more tightly than ever before. His father would have been so proud to see the birth of their baby boy into the world, a safe and secure world that Alexander had created for his family through pure effort and hard work. Cassandra held him tightly as she looked at their son, pondering a possible name, but distracted by the feeling of Alexander's nostalgia. She moved to look at him—

***

"I can't believe this, it's just another happy ending. You have no idea how tired I am of reading the same story over and over, it's driving me crazy," he practically yelled in exasperation, "Why are you doing this to me?"

I was livid. He had hardly given a chance to the story I presented, and then he skipped to the end. He hadn't done that before, so I knew he was really irritated over all of this, but not as much as I. He skipped all the best parts, including the heartbreak and loss that he so badly wanted to find in a piece of writing. He didn't even bother to look into the surrounding volumes to see the much darker path Alexander could have taken and the destruction and devastation that it would have left, which I knew would have brought him more satisfaction at the time, as sad as that may be. It was right there in front of him but he was so impatient and clueless he didn't even give it a chance.

It was almost as if he was losing all knowledge of the purpose of this place, forgetting the way stories could change and grow in any direction possible. My building anger drove me to want to hit him again, but it was clear to me that neither of us had the emotional capacity for a fight right now.

So, I tried to do something rational. He had his head resting in his hands, his coffee sitting cold on the table, so I took a stack of books and placed it in front of him, hoping that somewhere in there he would find something that interested him. He looked up slowly, a scowl on his face. "I want to do something else," he almost growled, but he knew that wasn't an option, and so did I. This was his purpose. Looking back, I suppose I sympathize with his exhaustion. He was just tired of his job.

He huffed for a few seconds more, before steeling himself upon sensing my anticipation. There had to be a story or two in there that would resonate with him, and I was dedicated not to stop until we had come to a resolution. There were a few of my absolute favorites in that stack, and I tried to hold a strong resolve not to get too upset if he tossed them to the side.

Frankly, I felt bad for those whose stories he was disregarding. Some people may live slow and predictable lives, but that doesn't mean they're menial or unimportant. I kept trying to rationalize his perspective within myself, but I was also offended, not just for the characters, but because he was treating my stories like they were trivial, as if each individual one wasn't a masterpiece within itself. I felt pride in each story, they all mattered to me equally, and the characters in each deserved recognition for the lives they were living. I tried to make sense of it all, and though I couldn't read his mind, I really hoped he was doing the same. He had a tendency to just be stubborn, so I couldn't tell.

Finally, after what seemed like an eternity of silence and thought—and it may as well have been—he picked up a book, the one on the top of the pile. It was the story of a young girl, elementary age, taking place two centuries after Alexander's story. He had been mostly interested in human stories as of late, if he was interested in anything at all, so that was primarily what I had put in his pile for the time being. The young girl was born into abundance and showered with gifts but struggled with making friends at school. One day she came home with cuts on her knees and confessed to her parents—

But it didn't matter. He put the book down after maybe ten minutes. This time, instead of yelling at me or sulking forever, he simply took a deep breath and reached out for his coffee. Before his hand could reach the handle, I swiftly pulled it away and replaced it with a hot cup, hoping it would encourage him to continue.

"Thank you," he said under his breath. He blew on the coffee for just a second before taking a sip and wincing a little as it burned his tongue. I felt slightly sympathetic, but I chose to do nothing, afraid to distract him from the task at hand.

Unprovoked, he picked up the next book in the pile. This one was very close to my heart, because I related to the main character here more than in other stories. She was a writer dealing with writer's block and facing heavy pressure from her publishing company to create another masterpiece, one she had yet to even start.

Once again, the librarian had no interest. He put it down before I even had the time to fully reconnect with the story and remember how she had been feeling throughout her life. But I did remember that she ended up happy after abandoning her career and instead dedicating her life and remaining funds to finding a hobby, which brought me joy. I suppose I don't know why I picked that story, probably just for my own enjoyment.

I took a moment though to remind myself of the alternate volumes in which she stayed at her job, and the mental darkness that followed, leading her to her grave. He would or would not have enjoyed it, I supposed, depending on the path he read into. Either way, I had hoped it would bring him a feeling of empathy, but in retrospect this was certainly not the place to start.

The librarian thoughtlessly sorted through the pile of books on the table, annoying me as he obviously judged them by their cover; such a cliche. He seemed to find no interest in the books I presented him with, but I saw a glimmer of motivation in his actions. He stood and began to meander amongst the aisles.

He rounded a corner, moving onto the next set of shelves, before suddenly stopping, catching me off guard as I watched him distantly. He picked up a particular book and studied it closely, taking in the artwork on the cover. It was an exceptionally unique cover which I had personally admired since it flew onto my shelf. The cover was blue, embossed with a silver moon with a cloud covering the bottom. The borders were decorated with oddly celestial vines. It looked as if the moon had designed it herself.

He stared at the cover for a long time, and I almost thought he was going to put it down in favor of a different story, but he flipped it over to read the back cover, something he had not done with the previous books. His eyes widened as he saw the main character. Even I had to admit, she was stunning, and the librarian always had a soft spot for aesthetics. It was undeniable that he was vain, shallow even, and I wondered to myself why I hadn't pulled this book out in the first place.

In retrospect, I should have figured right away that all he cared for was her looks. He read with no intention of rediscovering his connection to the literature, but rather so he could imagine a beautiful woman living her life as the pages designated. Reductive, yes, but to be expected I suppose.

He opened the book to the first page, and with a look of semi-genuine interest, started reading.

***

Birdie was bored. There was no better word to describe how she had felt about her life for the past months, years even. She tried many hobbies and paths, none of them satiating her longing for fulfillment, contentedness. She went to college and majored in theater, where she discovered she loved to perform but hated learning the rules and disciplines of performance. It was stupid to her that she had to be graded on her passion, so she left. She worked in a cafe for a while, only to discover that she was too introverted to care for the stories of random customers. It all got too repetitive too fast. She loved creating, so she opened one business, and then another, where she sold her art. But she quickly felt invalidated when people didn't immediately snatch up her pieces, feeling that her work wasn't good enough for anyone, and she closed the shops.

Here she stood, at the gateway to a new world—which was, in reality, the gate to an international plane—, giddy with nerves but also excitement. She was finally here and she was going to see the world.

She was ready to erase who she had been and create who she was meant to be. She was going to find her life.

***

The librarian kept reading.

B irdie was afraid of planes and flying, ironically so. Though she knew it was rare, there was always the possibility that the plane would go down, falling right out of the sky and crashing into the mountains, the ocean, or the seemingly endless fields of some place distant from home. They may look for her and never be able to find her, her memory would become lost to the world, unable to build a legacy.

She held on tightly to the straps of her bag as she showed her passport, scanned her boarding pass, and walked down the jetway towards the terrifying aircraft. 'Everything is gonna be fine,' she thought in a hushed inner voice, trying to ease her mind. She had flown countless times, having traveled a lot with her mother when she was young, but for some reason, it never got easier.

Her anxiety subsided a little as she sat in her seat and waited as the plane taxied down the runway, but it picked right back up as the plane sped down the tarmac and pulled up into the air. She was in a window seat and kept her eyes on the clouds the whole way up. She'd always thought that they were so beautiful, but there was something ominous to them as well.

She took deep breaths, trying for a moment to ignore the growing feeling of dread in her stomach. Anxiety or intuition, she didn't know, but something felt inescapably wrong. The clouds grew darker as the aircraft ascended, complimenting the building darkness in her thoughts and pushing all sense of safety out of her mind. She clasped her hands tightly, trying to calm herself but finding it impossible.

***

I saw the librarian take a deep breath, eyes chasing the words on the page. It made me want to giggle, seeing him try to blend into the story like a chameleon, but it ultimately took me aback. I was shocked to see him drawn into a story like that, enough that he would mindlessly mimic the actions of the main character. I watched hopefully as he read on.

***

Looking at the clouds may have been the worst thing she could have done. She would have preferred to have never seen it, and just let her anxiety tell her that an engine had gone out. She would never be able to rationalize what she saw in her final moments.

Deep in the clouds, a terrifying creature materialized from the dense darkness. The monster looked like it was part of the cloud itself, like it would be soft but impossible to touch. Its mouth was agape as it accelerated towards the plane, its three terrifying rows of teeth stole the attention away from the tiny red eyes burning high on its head.

Birdie froze, too terrified to make a sound. She was going to die, and she balled her hands into fists so tight that her nails cut into her palms. She clenched her jaw and braced for impact—

***

"Absolutely not," the librarian exclaimed in disbelief, quickly flipping through the rest of the book only to see that the remaining pages were blank, "What the hell was that?" I almost chuckled, as he had no one to blame but himself for the volume he chose.

It made me feel good, though, to see what seemed to be a glimmer of interest in his eyes, something I had not seen cross his features in what felt like ages. Though it had been only a short few paragraphs that he had thus far examined, I could see that he wasn't just reading, he was experiencing the story, as he was meant to. I felt proud of my work when he fully fell into it, and I smiled to myself. This was good for us.

I quickly grabbed a different volume off the shelf and placed it in front of him, not wanting him to lose interest before he continued. He rolled his eyes and looked at the equally beautiful cover. This book looked exactly the same, but there were no clouds over the moon, a sign of good fortune, apparently. He wasted no time in diving into the story.

***

She held on tightly to the straps of her bag as she scanned her boarding pass and walked down the jetway towards the terrifying aircraft. 'Everything is gonna be fine,' she thought in a hushed inner voice, trying to ease her mind. She had flown countless times, having traveled a lot with her mother when she was young, but for some reason, it never got easier.

Her anxiety subsided a little as she sat in her seat and waited as the plane taxied down the runway, but it picked right back up as the plane sped along the tarmac and pulled up into the air. She was in a window seat and kept her eyes on the clouds the whole way up. She'd always felt that they were so beautiful and something about them always felt so comforting, but she couldn't place why.

She kept her eyes on the clouds as the plane ascended through them, amazed by how they looked so soft and yet so intangible. She saw her reflection in the window as they passed through them, and was shocked to see her relaxed expression instead of the anxiety she was feeling inside. Maybe she was numb, but it didn't feel like that, it didn't feel like nothing. Maybe she was improving, at least she hoped, as that was the primary purpose of her trip.

Birdie looked at this moment as a good opportunity to nurture her growth. The anxiety had never served her, and in this moment she recognized that it was causing her only harm. She felt a pain in her chest and a heaviness in her heart, so she took some intentional breaths and tried to reset to a state of comfort and calm. She kept looking at the clouds as she did, now so far below the plane that she had to crane her neck a little bit to see them—but there they were, beautiful and bright and comforting. The sunny, shining sky above them heavily contrasted the gloomy weather that hid underneath, and she smiled at the juxtaposition.

She took a moment to remind herself why she was putting herself through all this anxiety to begin with. She had always dreamt of going to London, and she was finally making it happen for herself, she had finally made her dreams come true. These thoughts helped to calm her mind and she closed her eyes and allowed herself to drift off to sleep.

The airport was huge and confusing, but Birdie was able to navigate it without too much issue. She tried to find her way to the bus like she had originally planned, but was feeling too overwhelmed, so she just called for a cab. She counted her breaths periodically, praising herself for mentally surviving the plane ride and landing safely at her destination.

The view out of the cab was breathtaking. Tears welled up in her eyes as she watched the reflection of the city lights twinkle along the ripples of the Thames, contrasting the starless sky above. It was wide and beautiful, and she felt truly awestruck. It was hard to remind herself that she was actually there, not just dreaming. No matter how much she pinched herself, it wouldn't do the trick. She tried different grounding techniques along the car ride, still taking deep breaths and mindfully following her thoughts. She hoped to be fully present when she arrived at the hostel, as she wanted to put her best foot forward with the new people she was about to meet.

***

I could tell that the librarian was having some second thoughts about this story. He wasn't all that interested in those surrounding mental health and self-improvement, which was ironic, given his obviously volatile headspace. He felt they moved too slowly, and I think he was uncomfortable with having the importance and practicality of self-care presented as a given. If I had known how much work the librarian himself needed, I might have led him towards reading stories centered on mental growth earlier in our time together, but I hadn't thought it necessary. He'd have to try to figure something out for himself, but he was too stubborn, and even potentially narcissistic.

He looked up from the pages for a moment as he sighed, and I worried that he was losing his gusto. It wasn't my job to get into a scuffle with him over his stubbornness, so I tried to just keep pushing him in the right direction. I put a piece of tiramisu, his favorite dessert, down next to his coffee as quickly as I could, and he muttered a brief "Thanks," before taking a bite. He savored the flavor for a moment before he finally looked back down at the words in his hands.

***

Birdie felt her anxiety seeping back in as she stood at the threshold of the hostel. She had probably been standing there for only a minute or two, but each second felt like an eternity. She couldn't explain it, but she felt a pit in her stomach and she was nervous to knock on the door. She wanted nothing more than to find a community in this new place, as she was afraid of being all alone in a new city, a new country at that.

Finally, she lifted her hand and knocked gently on the door. Too gently, it seemed, because she heard no movement on the other side. She waited a moment, then knocked again, louder this time. She heard some rustling through the door, and within moments it was opening. She was greeted by a beautiful and friendly face with a smile plastered across it.

"Hi!" the girl said excitedly, "I'm Emma! You must be Birdie?" Birdie smiled. It wasn't a huge deal, but she was happy to have been expected.

"Yeah, hi," she replied, sounding more timid than she meant to, "Sorry I arrived so late, I got a little lost outside."

"Oh don't worry about it! We all got lost when we first got here, you're not alone," Emma said with a smile. Though they were throwaway words, hearing that she wasn't alone meant a lot to Birdie, as she was afraid that she would be.

"Oh my gosh, I don't want to keep you waiting there, come inside, warm up!" Birdie stepped into her temporary home, thankful for the warmth in the chill of early spring. Emma was so welcoming, but for some reason, Birdie was starting to get a feeling in her gut that she was being treated disingenuously. She tried to ignore this feeling, chalking it up to anxiety and memories of the negative experiences in her past. She had a bad habit of ignoring her gut feelings.

The next half hour was spent on introductions and short conversations as she got to know the barest minimum about everyone she was staying with, forgetting half of their names in the process. That time was followed by another half hour of unpacking, just enough to make her sleeping space comfortable, as there was no room anywhere for her to put away her clothes. That was alright though, she had come prepared to live out of her suitcase.

The girls took her to dinner that night, wanting to show her a bit of the neighborhood. There was enriching conversation throughout the meal and it was clear that there were strong friendships already established upon her arrival. She felt included, but not as much as she had hoped, and her anxiety crept back up again; she was afraid of feeling alienated in her new environment.

***

The librarian frowned briefly, and I saw a distinct expression of understanding, a certain glint in his eye that I had only seen before on rare occasion. He didn't want to feel alienated either, which seemed to be an instinctive want, as he had never had a community to be alienated from. Aside from me, that is, but no matter how much he got on my nerves, I thought I could never push him away.

***

Her first night in the hostel was sleepless, as she couldn't quiet her restless thoughts. This was not how she wanted to feel upon being in this new space, and she was afraid that the feeling would not go away—a self-fulfilling prophecy. She dedicated her energy to planning things she could do alone in the city, so she didn't feel so let down if she wasn't able to build the friendships she wanted to with the time she had there. By the time others started to rise in the morning, she had an extensive list saved in her phone of destinations to explore and excursions nearby.

T he next few days went by in a blur, and she noticed that she felt dissociated more often than not. The feeling that she was dreaming wasn't subsiding, and she felt alone even when the hostel was at its liveliest. The longer she was there, the less time of day she was receiving from those she lived with; they were already too close to one another to make room for her in the group dynamic.

She tried hard to practice mindfulness, but she couldn't tell if she was really being distanced from them or if her anxiety was altering her perception of the situation around her, causing her to distance herself. She thought about it long and hard, but really couldn't understand the difference. She felt sad and lonely and was desperate for friendship in this foreign environment. Her list of destinations was largely untouched, and she beat herself up over being too lost in overanalysis to get out there and enjoy her holiday.

***

The librarian put the book down in frustration. He was unhappy, and at first, I couldn't tell why. I knew that this story was maybe a little too slow-paced for him, but it would pick up in no time if he could only stick it out.

But through his frustration, I saw something growing. I could sense a change in him, a slight reversion to his previous self. Though he was feeling negative, his features had softened, and there was a shimmer of light in his eyes. I felt joyful; my efforts seemed to be making a difference.

"I think I understand her... I-" he said quietly. My thoughts stopped in their tracks. I waited for him to elaborate, but he seemed to withdraw.

Regardless, I felt excited and slightly triumphant upon hearing that lone sentence. I racked my brain for what might be so special about Birdie to make him relate to her like that. I think that—though he so thoroughly disregarded and bottled his own feelings—he understood her mindset. He was longing for companionship and understanding, something he was completely incapable of receiving from anyone but myself. In truth, I wasn't always the best company, so I felt for him.

I was moved by his feelings of empathy for Birdie, so I went back to the shelves and picked another volume. If he was to live vicariously through her for the duration of this story, then I wanted him to feel some positivity for himself. Birdie deserved to feel that too. We both knew well enough that she was going to feel all of this anyway, but I thought it would be better to experience it firsthand. I hoped that this volume would put the librarian into a better headspace.

He looked up as I set the book down gently on the coffee table in front of him, a puzzled look on his face. He knew as well as I that this was a rare gesture; he expected me to have him stick it out with the version he was holding, but I knew this one suited him better. He took a breath for a moment, and then picked up the book.

***

The girls took her to dinner that night, wanting to show her a bit of the neighborhood. There was enriching conversation throughout the meal, and it was clear that there were strong friendships already established upon her arrival, but she felt included anyway. Emma was very inviting right off the bat, asking Birdie questions about her background, reasons for travel, and many others to try to get to know her and build a stronger connection. Birdie felt that she fit right in, and with Emma's help, she was able to create great foundations for friendship as soon as she landed.

The next day, Emma took Birdie to a nearby museum, where Birdie was amazed by the collection and variety of the displayed art. There was a special gallery for a guest artist: a mix of graphic design with seemingly mundane pieces of photography. Birdie found herself standing in front of different pieces for minutes at a time, allowing herself to take in every nuance of the artwork, constantly finding new details that were unique and beautiful. She tried to find meaning in them for herself, without reading the descriptions of the artist's purpose. After all, art is meant to make people feel things, and she wanted to discover what feelings came up for her before delving into the artistic intentions.

One piece in particular stuck out to her: a photograph of a woman standing on the ledge of a cliff over what Birdie imagined was originally the sea, but it had been graphically altered into the cosmos of space. Constellations littered the expanse below her, with ripples of galaxies lapping up onto the shore. The cliff was not too high, and Birdie wondered what it would feel like to jump down into that vast expanse of space.

She related to the woman in the photograph. Birdie was standing on the edge of a great expanse, and if she jumped she didn't know what was waiting for her over the edge. At the same time, though, she felt as though she had already taken the leap. Coming to a foreign country was a huge achievement in and of itself, and she was unequivocally proud of herself.

Emma was feeling tired after their time in the museum and decided to go home, but Birdie still felt full of energy and wasn't ready to head back quite yet. She took herself to a cozy cafe with her mostly empty journal and a pep in her step. Birdie had a great love for stationery, and was thankful for her expansive collection of floral and nature-based stickers and washi tapes for the rare occasions that she felt like opening up to the pages of her journal. It was something she wished she did more often, as she always felt that her thoughts were more organized after writing them down. Having decided to go with a pink and rosy theme for these few pages, she decorated the corners and edges with accents that inspired her to write her contented thoughts of the day.

She tried to focus her thoughts on her mental state, attempting to thoroughly log the structure of her thinking as she had learned to do through years of therapy. She wrote about how her thoughts that day were productive and that she didn't feel dragged down by the potential of negative outcomes, but instead was motivated by the positivity of her day. She wrote that she was feeling fulfilled, and that, since her arrival, her boredom had substantially subsided. She was happy, and she was going to continue to chase this feeling.

***

The librarian set down the book for a moment as he finished his tiramisu. He had a thoughtful look about him, and I could see that he was trying to process Birdie's feelings. Feelings he, ironically, pushed down but seemingly wanted to experience; as far as I could tell, fulfillment was not something he was familiar with. It made me sad for a moment.

He, just as much as anyone in any of these stories, deserved access to the full range of emotion and experience, but he was unfortunately deprived of that. I didn't know for sure, but I was fairly certain that this path was not one that he had chosen. Much like me, he just began here one day, knowing nothing for certain but that meant to stay here indefinitely. I knew he was okay with it at first, a domestic acceptance of circumstance, but as time led up to this moment, it became more apparent to both of us that he longed for more, and he deserved more as well. I didn't feel the same, I was more than happy with my purpose, but I think I would have felt more whole if I had a less torn companion.

He sat in thought for a long time. It seemed like he wanted to go to sleep, though we both knew he didn't need it. It looked like he was just at a point where he was ready for a break, for time to process what he was reading and how he was relating to it. It would probably be good for him if he was capable of sleep, I thought. He deserved to recharge. He deserved a more human experience in general, and I knew he wanted it based on how much time he spent reading stories from Earth.

I wanted to ask if he was okay as the silence dragged on, but I knew he would speak up if he wasn't. He was always willing to make his unhappiness known, especially if it was about a story I presented to him. I just wanted him to speak, to say anything, because as talented as I had become at reading his face, I could never read his mind. The contortions of his facial features made me wish I could... But the silence continued.

***

Birdie found a small restaurant and sat down for yet another delicious meal. Though she was happy with her already budding friendships, her time alone was extremely important to her, and she was perfectly content to eat alone. She smiled to herself between every bite, thankful for the day she had. She was afraid that it would be a struggle to find things to do or experiences to have when she arrived, but she had found herself happy in a foreign place the day after her arrival, which she took as an achievement.

She was tired after the meal and found her way home, though, admittedly, she missed a few turns along the way. She didn't view getting lost as negative, she instead took it as an opportunity to familiarize herself with the area surrounding her hostel. She spent about half an hour exploring the area and noticed several cute cafes and corner shops that she wanted to visit. She made a note on her phone with a checklist of them, not wanting to miss out on or forget any of them.

When she finally arrived home, about half of the girls were sitting in the common area, drinking tea and chatting. One of them, Bre, was quietly sitting in the corner reading a book, but she beckoned Birdie over as soon as she saw her. Birdie approached, slightly apprehensive since she and Bre had only talked a little over dinner at this point.

"How was your first day?" Bre asked, and she seemed genuinely interested.

"It was really good," Birdie said plainly, but she elaborated after taking a breath and reminding herself that there was nothing to be hesitant about, she wanted to build connections.

"I tagged along with Emma to an art museum today," Birdie said, trying to find her footing in the conversation, "There was this piece... on the surface, it seemed so... simple. But it was beautiful. I haven't connected with a piece like that in a long time."

Birdie went quiet for a moment, but Bre signaled her to continue, "Go on," she said.

"Okay, um..." Birdie hesitated, unsure if she was ready to share the connection she felt to the piece, "Well, it was of a woman. She was standing on the edge of a cliff, and I think she was ready to jump. Dark, I know, but she was standing above this expanse of space, I don't think she would have fallen hard. I actually think that she would have floated. She would have been able to explore the galaxies and stars and sun... and that's how I feel I guess. I finally got out of the nest and I'm exploring and living in what's around me. I know it's only been a day... but I just... I think I understand her."

***

I smiled to myself. The connection between the librarian and Birdie was becoming more and more apparent, as she echoed the words he had uttered mere moments ago. I made no moves to point this out, just observing in silence.

***

Birdie surprised herself with how easily she opened her heart to Bre, even through her pauses and stutters. Bre listened to Birdie intently, and she saw care and attention behind her bright eyes. She continued.

Birdie told Bre about the adorable cafes and shops she had passed in her exploration, and Bre responded excitedly when hearing the name of her favorite shop. She told Bre about everything except the self-therapeutic journaling she had done, which felt too personal for her to share with anyone. Bre listened intently, seeming like she sincerely wanted to soak in every word.

The girls welcomed Birdie into their conversation, giving her a warm cup of peppermint tea to help her wind down from her day. It seemed that they loved to talk about boys because they each had exciting stories of spice, love, and drama with both local boys and guys on vacation alike. Though Birdie was not altogether too interested in the gossip, she was happy to be included.

That night in bed, Birdie looked over the list of destinations she had cultivated on her walk, and added more that she found online, excited to see as much as she possibly could in her time abroad. She found countless museums, historical sites, and restaurants with lots of buzz that excited her; it was more than enough to fill her time. She just had to make sure she kept herself as motivated as possible in the time she had allotted for her trip.

She felt genuinely happy.

***

At this point, the librarian took a proper break. He found himself some peppermint tea before I had the chance to realize he wanted it, and took himself to the window, where he gazed out into the perpetual dawn. He still had that thoughtful look across his face, and I thought I saw a small smile crossing his features. Perhaps he had connected to Birdie more than I expected; this empathy was not something I predicted would come so easily.

"She's... she's growing," I was shocked to hear him speak, but I was ready to listen, "But she used to be... well, she used to be like me. I want to feel that." His introspection was apparent, and I was thankful that he chose to finally elaborate. At the same time though, I was having a hard time believing him. He had shown no intention of growth in a long time, perhaps ever. Feelings and habits... He might as well be human. I wished in this moment that I could say something in response, but I knew he understood my silence.

We sat quietly for a while more. He even closed his eyes, and I thought he might be mimicking sleep, but his eyes opened after a while. He stared again at that moment before the sunrise, the colors dancing across the horizon in a silent rhythm. I just watched him, trying to read his expression as I always did. I hadn't seen him so intentionally quiet, so thoughtful, in a while and I wanted to enjoy it while it lasted, but I also wanted to understand his process better.

I'm not sure how long we sat in silence before he moved back to pick up the book. He seemed to be enjoying the dawn because he brought the book away from the coffee table and over to his seat by the window. He took a moment to run his fingers over the chrome cover, taking in every detail like he was going to be tested on it. I wanted to smile as he opened the pages again.

**

Birdie tapped her foot nervously, sipping her coffee. The caffeine was unnecessary, as the anxious energy already filling her was causing her leg to bounce on its own. She looked up and caught the barista's eyes again, and again they both looked away blushing. She hadn't felt this nervous to talk to someone in so long, and they hadn't even spoken yet.

Internally, she thanked herself for walking past this cafe on her first full day in town, and for writing it down on her list of places she wanted to visit. The atmosphere was cozy and comforting, a rustic vibe with plants hanging across the ceiling and adorning every corner, raw brick walls, and fairy lights strung across the naked beams on the ceiling. She sat in a quiet nook in a slate gray armchair tucked into a corner next to the window. Dusk had fallen, and she watched as the colors faded into darker hues of blue and purple.

She wanted to know his name. Though her view was partially obstructed by a coffee grinder, she could tell that he had a beautiful smile from the way his eyes scrunched as he talked to customers. His eyes had depth and dimension, hazel with a brighter green surrounding the pupil and darker browns adorning the edges of the iris. They were entrancing. The way he looked at her made her feel like she was in high school, butterflies dancing through her and making her feel all warm inside. She smiled into her coffee, trying to hide it in case he was looking; she didn't want to drop her cool, though she didn't know why she was putting on a front in the first place.

She looked back to her journal, feeling partially satisfied with the blue theme of stickers and highlights with which she had decorated the corners of the pages, but wanting to add something more. It felt too two-dimensional, but she continued with her writing anyway. She wanted to journal about all the experiences she'd had over the past few days but was too distracted by the butterflies she was feeling, so she wrote about that instead.

She quickly closed her journal, perhaps too quickly, as the barista walked up to her and took the seat across from her in the little nook.

"You free to chat for a minute?" he asked with a grin. He had taken down his mask, and Birdie was correct, his smile was stunning.

"Yeah, sure, but aren't you working?" she asked shyly, not wanting to get him into trouble.

"Don't worry about it, I'm on break," he said, still grinning. She couldn't help but smile herself, his positivity was infectious, and his smooth accent made her feel bright inside. He was exceptionally handsome, and she couldn't place her finger on just why he would want to talk to her of all people. But that was her insecurity talking.

Realistically, Birdie was very beautiful. Her brown eyes shone like stars, and the freckles dotted across her face were complimentary constellations. She had been called stunning her whole life, but, just like now, she didn't quite believe it.

Their conversation was surface-level throughout his short break, just general get-to-knows, but she was more than happy to entertain. She learned that his name was Leon, he was 25, and he had lived in a town a few hours out before moving to the city earlier that year. She happily answered all his questions, and couldn't help but giggle when he asked so seriously what her favorite color was.

This cafe quickly became her favorite. She found herself seated in that armchair more than she expected to, always looking forward to the playful eye contact she would share with Leon. He'd always come to her on his break, like clockwork, distracting her from her train of thought as she journaled. He seemed to really love having her attention on him because as she became more and more of a regular, he'd do more things to catch her attention across the room. One night, when business was winding down and there were few people in the seating area, he caught her attention by juggling some oranges behind the counter, causing her to almost choke on her latte.

M ore than a month had passed since Birdie's arrival, and she had become very comfortable with the neighborhood surrounding her hostel. As she walked past the cafe one night, heading home from dinner, she jumped in surprise as Leon caught her arm. "Hi!" he said, a bounce in his voice. He sounded out of breath, and she realized he had run a bit to catch up to her before she had gotten too far out of his sight.

"Hi!" she giggled in response, trying to match his energy.

"I don't know what you're doing tonight," he started boldly, "but I work until ten, do you want to go out with me somewhere afterward?"

"So late?" Birdie questioned, "Is anything even open then?"

"Yes! There's a couple of clubs I love, or if that isn't your vibe we could go to another cafe, I know a few that are open 24 hours!" Birdie was flattered by his eagerness. She was still trying to keep her cool around him for some reason, but the invitation made her giddy and she was certain that her blush was giving that away.

"A club sounds nice," she said, nervously, "I actually haven't been to one before." A look of shock crossed Leon's face, but it was quickly replaced by excitement. They made their plans to meet around eleven so Leon could have enough time to get ready after work, and Birdie went in for just a moment to get a coffee to make sure she wouldn't fall asleep before then. She was brimming with nervous, excited energy as she walked away and he looked after her with a smile.

Eleven o'clock came faster than expected, and Birdie did everything she could in the time leading up to meeting Leon to make sure she looked and felt exceptionally confident. She didn't really have any club-worthy clothes, seeing as she hadn't really expected to be going to any, so Emma let her borrow something cute. She wore a sparkly black knee-length dress with a slit up one thigh and some boots that went up almost to the end of the dress. She already had a coat that matched pretty well, a lightly fluffy black zip-up. Emma and Bre helped her with her makeup, which she rarely wore; she did her best to hold her face still as they put on some sharp but small winged eyeliner, light glitter on her eyelids, and deep red lipstick. She almost didn't recognize herself in the mirror, but she felt amazing.

Thankfully, it wasn't too cold outside, and Leon got back to the cafe just a few minutes after she did, so she hardly had to wait. He was dressed in a different aesthetic from Birdie's, but they complimented each other well. He wore black cargo pants and a band t-shirt, and she couldn't help but to admire; he was even more handsome out of uniform. He treated her very casually as soon as he arrived, pulling her in for a hug and kissing her gently on the cheek. She knew he could see that she was blushing as they pulled away, and he immediately flashed her that stunning smile.

He filled her in on some information about the club as they walked in that direction; apparently, it wasn't any more than a fifteen-minute walk away from the cafe. She wondered how she had missed it on her walks, but understood as soon as they arrived, as it was advertised by a neon sign that only lit up at night and the club itself was down a set of stairs into the basement of the building. They flashed their IDs at the door and were given stamps on the backs of their hands for reentry throughout the night if needed.

The music was unbelievably loud, and the DJ played a variety of genres, though it was all pretty upbeat and around the same BPM. Birdie didn't have much experience going out, so when Leon asked what she wanted to drink she said to surprise her. He went right up to the bar and came back with a vodka drink for himself and a rum and orange juice for her. She took one sip and her eyes widened, it was delicious and she could hardly taste the alcohol. They made their way through the accumulating crowd over to an open booth at the back of the club, where they sat for a while sipping their drinks.

***

Hoping to add some further immersion, I put on a song from that generation in Birdie's timeline, perhaps a bit too loud. The librarian leaped out of his seat, the book falling onto the floor and skidding off a few feet.

"Shut that the fuck off!" he shouted, and I laughed internally. It seemed I had done the opposite of what I intended, but it was worth it for the reaction. The frustration that he had been expressing towards me earlier seemed to have faded, as his words were fueled by shock and I didn't feel their usual sting.

I turned the music off, but not before watching the librarian with his hands over his ears for a few moments, eyes searching for mine in vain so as to shoot me a glare. When the quiet finally returned, the librarian picked up the book, sat back down, and took a deep breath to try to bring himself back into the right headspace. I brought him a cocktail to help regain his interest, and he chuckled in appreciation.

***

Birdie loved people-watching, but she only had a second to do so before the butterflies in her stomach came back as Leon boldly wrapped his arm around her waist, pulling her closer to him. She leaned into him before turning her head to see a look on his face that she hadn't seen before. His eyes were darkening and it drew her into a trance. They didn't even have one full drink between them, but Birdie surprised herself and leaned in to kiss him. He kissed back, softly at first. He threaded his hand gently through her hair, and she leaned into the feeling.

She hadn't been kissed like this in a long time, and though she felt exposed being surrounded by so many people, she didn't for a second want it to stop. She put her hand onto his waist and lazily dragged her fingers over his torso as he started pulling her in for a deeper kiss before abruptly pulling away. He ran his hand over her jaw and held it in his hand for a moment as he bit his lip. Birdie could only imagine that her lipstick had already smudged all around her mouth, but she couldn't tell from his expression.

After a moment of silence and another brief but heated kiss, they started to talk to one another over their drinks, though more accurately they were yelling, trying to hear one another over the bumping music. Leon pulled out a pack of cigarettes as they spoke, and offered one to Birdie. She really wasn't a smoker, but she accepted and put it delicately between her lips. His eyes twinkled as he did the same with his own, before putting his hand back onto her jaw, guiding her face so the tips of their cigarettes could be lit by the same flame. It wasn't her first cigarette, but the first puff made her cough a little nonetheless and she felt embarrassed. Leon laughed, but it wasn't condescending; he thought she was cute.

Birdie finally took a moment to people-watch as she leaned back into Leon's chest, enjoying the way it felt to have his arm wrapped so tightly around her. She drank more quickly than expected, and soon Leon pulled her up to get another, but not before carefully wiping away the lipstick that was smudged around her mouth, as she had suspected.

She wanted something stronger this time around, and he suggested that they just do a few shots. Birdie was more than happy with the idea, and Leon ordered a set of four tequila shots for the two of them. They threw them back quickly, clinking their glasses before each one. He kissed her again right at the bar, harder this time than the last, before taking her hand and pulling her onto the dance floor.

Birdie didn't think she had ever danced like this before. It flowed so naturally and comfortably as she moved her hips to the heavy rhythm of the song, relishing in the feeling of a strong pair of hands on her waist as she did so. She felt the alcohol beginning to distract her and closed her eyes through moments of kissing Leon as they danced. He moved his hands up and down her body and she melted into the touch, feeling euphoric under the neon lights.

She discovered that it was easier than she thought to get free drinks, after all, she was exceptionally beautiful and the men surrounding her seemed to care for that above all else. It appeared that Leon loved to watch her swindle them, reminding himself that he was the one lucky enough to take her out for the night.

The free drinks throughout the night left her with a warm and loose feeling and she stumbled a bit on her walk back across the club to Leon in the booth. He pulled her into his lap when she made her way over, kissing her on the neck as she sat there. She rolled her head back to give him access, dropping all her inhibitions.

When he whispered to her that they should go back to his place she was quick to agree, and, though he was quite drunk himself, he gave her his arm as she adjusted to standing back up. They shared a light over a cigarette as they stood outside the club, exchanging drunk flirty looks, which turned filthy as they began walking back in the direction of the cafe, towards Leon's place.

It was a small studio apartment, and Birdie hardly had a moment to take it all in before Leon pressed her against the wall and kissed her passionately. She leaned into it, with no feeling of her usual reservations or anxiety. He moved to her jaw, then down her neck, stopping for a moment as he moved aside the straps on her shoulders and pulled down the neckline of her dress. She threw her head back as he kissed her shoulders, almost having forgotten the feeling of this kind of intimacy.

The night moved quickly, partially thanks to the alcohol running through them. Their bodies wound together so familiarly as they undressed one another, taking in the sights in front of them. Birdie couldn't help but reach out her hand and stroke it over his abs as he pulled his shirt over his head, her breath taken away upon seeing the definition. But she didn't have much time to be awestruck as he lowered himself over her again, kissing her deeply.

They let out a harmony of moans, and Birdie closed her eyes as she took in the feeling. She hadn't made love in a long time, though this felt less than that, but she was enthralled nonetheless. Though she was drunk, she made sure to stay present and experience their time together with all of her senses.

Birdie vaguely remembered falling asleep, but felt happy as she woke up next to Leon. He was still sleeping soundly, so she took a moment to take a proper and sober look around his little studio. The bed was placed in the corner by the window, looking out onto the city, though most of the view was of a brick wall as the apartment wasn't on a very high level. There were three steps up from the bedroom into the living area, which was crowded with a loveseat, a small television, and a kitchenette. It was small, but very cozy. She saw an espresso machine on the counter but didn't feel at home enough to help herself.

She watched Leon sleep for a while, trying to decide if it would be okay to wake him, but she decided against it for the time being. She did really want a coffee, and decided it would be best for her to take herself to a cafe or back to the hostel to get some. Her hangover wasn't the worst she had had, but it was uncomfortable nonetheless, and she hoped some caffeine would help.

After a little more thought, she decided to wake Leon, but just enough to say goodbye. She lightly shook his shoulder, quietly saying his name. He groaned as he blinked his eyes open, obviously still very tired.

"Good morning," Birdie said lightheartedly, "I think I'm gonna head home, I need a coffee." Leon only groaned in response, before rolling over in bed and hugging his pillow to his chest. Birdie had to admit that it annoyed her, especially after the previous night, but she chalked it up to the hangover and tried not to take it to heart. She dressed herself, suddenly regretting the outfit choice as she'd have to find her way home in broad daylight wearing that dress and those boots. She went to the restroom quickly before leaving and discovered that he had left a hickey above one of her breasts, causing her cheeks to flush in embarrassment. She quickly zipped up her jacket before walking out onto the street.

B irdie made her way to her favorite cafe the
next day, looking forward to seeing Leon,
though slightly annoyed that they hadn't had any
communication since their night together. She had
sent him one text, just to check in on how he was
handling the hangover, but she hadn't gotten any
response. She took her usual spot by the window when
she arrived, but was immediately taken aback when she
got to the counter to order.

Leon was standing right there at the register, but
when she smiled at him he looked at her like a stranger.
He asked for her order with a bland tone in his voice,
and Birdie ordered more timidly than she originally
intended, upset with the encounter. He made no
effort for further communication, making her drink
and calling her name when it was ready. He didn't

stand there with her drink like he usually did, he just left it on the counter for her to pick up.

Birdie was hurt, and she couldn't explain the sudden change. Had she said something wrong when they were drunk? Was he just an asshole? All the possibilities ran through her head in a spiral, distracting her from her journaling, though she realized that these feelings were probably what she should be writing about. She drank her coffee much faster than usual and ignored the stationery as she journaled, trying to just get her feelings onto the page and get out of there. She was annoyed and frustrated, not wanting to feel unwelcome in a space that had previously felt safe to her, but she didn't want to be in Leon's sight either. She wrote that she felt embarrassed, upset, and confused; she couldn't place what in the world would cause such a sudden shift.

***

The librarian closed the book, frustrated once again. His tea had long since gone cold, the cocktail polished off; he didn't make an effort to reach for either.

"I would... I mean I could never do that to her," he said quietly. He had put words to his frustrations, though I had already inferred what he was thinking. I started to wonder again why he had continued with this story. Was it because he related to her, or was it something deeper? I wished at that moment that I could ask. I was happy to see the librarian's emotions evoked by something outside of himself, but I felt concern begin to creep in for which I couldn't find the origin.

He sat in awkward silence for a while more, before he stood and made his way over to the shelf. It took him a little while to find the story without my help, walking up and down a couple of wrong aisles, but he got there eventually. He ran his pointer finger over the bindings of the massive series, starting at the point of the last volume I had given him, trying to intuitively pick where he should go from there. He was obviously unhappy with the direction the story had taken, and I wondered for another moment if it was for the sake of Birdie or for his own personal comfort.

He pulled a volume, once again with a very similar cover, and I could see a look cross his face, one of hope. But something felt... off; it struck me as selfish. My concern heightened, but I watched as he sat down and began to read.

***

She watched Leon sleep for a while, trying to decide if it would be okay to wake him, but she decided against it for the time being. She did really want a coffee, and decided it would be best for her to take herself to a cafe or back to the hostel to get some. Her hangover wasn't the worst she had had, but it was uncomfortable nonetheless, and she hoped some caffeine would help.

After a little more thought, she decided to wake Leon, but just enough to say goodbye. She lightly shook his shoulder, quietly saying his name. He groaned as he blinked his eyes open, obviously still very tired.

"Good morning," Birdie said lightheartedly, "I think I'm gonna head home, I need a coffee." Leon's eyes opened slightly wider and he reached out and lightly grabbed her arm before pulling her on top of him, wrapping her into his arms. He groaned a sleepy "Good morning," as he held her tightly. She felt so safe and comfortable in his arms, and it was hard not to melt right into his touch. "Let me make you a coffee here," he said, still groggy. She smiled and allowed herself to lean into him fully before nodding in agreement.

They laid like that for a few minutes more before Leon roused himself enough to go to the small kitchen. Seeing as he was a barista, he was used to quality, complex drinks, so he had invested in a small espresso machine. Birdie was thankful for this, as it would make for a much better morning than the instant coffee in her hostel. She watched him happily as he made lattes for the two of them, adding vanilla, which he knew she liked based on her past orders at his cafe.

She moved to get dressed as the realization suddenly hit her that she was still just sitting naked, but was immediately distracted as Leon ran to his dresser. He pulled out a pair of black sweatpants and a huge t-shirt from another band that he liked, and he gave her a deep kiss as he passed them to her. She smiled into his lips and looked at him with stars in her eyes as he returned to their lattes. The drinks were ready by the time she was dressed and he carefully brought them over to the bed where he sat with her. As she sipped, she noticed that he had carefully folded her dress and set it on top of his dresser, and he gently placed her jacket on the rail of his small set of stairs as well. She blushed at the gesture.

***

I saw the librarian smile to himself, and my concern faded, partially. It felt good to see him so connected to a story, so interested that it affected him like this. It was clear that he felt an extreme connection to Birdie, and I felt a sense of achievement at having brought him a story that we could actually enjoy together. He finally looked up, seeming to be in a better headspace than he had been in earlier. He looked out at the dawn, and I brought him a vanilla latte, something to help him become more immersed in the story; his facial expressions once again showed me that he was thankful.

***

Birdie and Leon laid together in bed all day, both happy for his day off. He seemed more well-adjusted to having a hangover than she, and made efforts to care for her as she rested. She felt so confident and comfortable around him and couldn't stop thinking about how grateful she was that he had been working in that cafe the day she first went in. Their connection came so easily, and it was equally apparent on both sides that they were enamored by one another.

They made love again, and this time that's what it actually felt like. They were sober, more connected, and more intimate than the last time. It was slower and gentler and they kissed deeply, both feeling lucky to have one another in that way.

The day turned into night, and they were still in one another's arms, watching the sunset in the small sliver of sky through his little window. She texted Emma to let her know that she wouldn't be home for yet another night, not wanting them to worry about her absence, and set her phone to the side.

***

I didn't think much of it at the time, but I saw the corner of the librarian's lip curl downward. He quickly covered it with a sip of his latte, and I let the gesture pass me by.

T he next few days felt like a blur. Birdie went to Leon's cafe whenever he was working, and he would boldly kiss her cheek when he gave her her drink, causing her to blush every time. Her journal steadily filled with pages of colorful stickers and stationery, partnered with joyful words to express the bright feelings she was experiencing. She smiled to herself as she wrote, her happiness apparent to anyone who gave her more than a glance. Leon continued to look at her with the same excitement that he did when she first started coming to the cafe, and she, of course, did the same.

Their first official date was romantic and undeniably aesthetically attractive; Leon packed them a traditional wicker picnic basket full of fruits, cheeses, a baguette, and a bottle of prosecco. They sat in a park by the

Thames, enjoying the green of the beautiful spring and effectively ignoring the brown tint of the river. They talked for endless hours about their interests and joys in life, much deeper conversation than they had initially had in their first cafe meeting. She noticed in the daylight that his hair had a warm, golden tint, something she couldn't really see through the brown in all the time they had spent together so far.

Everything she learned about him was interesting to her, even the things that one might find to be more mundane. It was, she thought, just because she was excited to be getting to know him. Having a chance to get to know someone so intimately was rare for her; it was something she hadn't pursued much, so she was more than happy to take in the new feeling.

Their dates out and nights in became more of a constant as the time passed, and she pushed the thoughts of their time running out to the back of her mind; her time there was limited, and, though she was still less than halfway through her trip, she didn't want to think about it ending.

Emma was extremely interested in Birdie's relationship and hounded her with questions on the now rare occasion that Birdie would come home. She was more than happy to answer, as she could say endless positive things about her budding relationship. Leon was good to her, treated her with the utmost respect, communicated with her kindly whenever they disagreed, and looked at her like she was the most beautiful girl in the world. She told her roommate all of these things as Emma listened in awe, envious of the connection Birdie had been able to find so quickly upon beginning her holiday.

***

I saw that slight frown again, and this time I didn't let it go without a thought. Something seemed wrong, but still, I couldn't place my finger on exactly what it might be.

The librarian was entranced by the book, devouring each word as he sipped the latte, which, as his face showed, it seemed he had developed a distaste for. His look of positivity was fading with each word he read, and more of a concerned and frustrated expression crossed his face. I couldn't explain it at the time, but I started to feel that I certainly made a mistake by placing this series in front of him.

While his expression showed all those emotions, it also showed a sure sense of empathy, which I used to comfort myself. I surely couldn't have made such a huge mistake, it was just another book after all. But it seemed as though he had dark thoughts running through his mind, thoughts I couldn't begin to comprehend through his facial expressions. I silently begged once again for him to say something, anything, that would give me an insight into his thoughts, but he was silent. Silent again.

***

Birdie sat in a quiet cafe, sipping an iced milk tea and swiping through social media. Leon sat beside her with his head on her shoulder, lightly dozing. They were not in their usual cafe, as it was his day off and he didn't want to spend it in his workplace. They had gone clubbing the night before and he was exhausted, as was she, but her hangover was much less intense this time; she didn't let herself get as excessively wasted as she did on their first night out together. She had offered to spend the day in bed, but he insisted that they get out to a cafe, knowing that she wanted to.

She turned to kiss him on the forehead, causing him to smile in his half-asleep state. She smiled in response, just so comfortable with him by her side, and happy she could be there for him to rest his tired head.

They sat like that for a while longer before he reached his hands to the sky and stretched as he let out a yawn; it seemed his hangover had finally subsided enough for him to open his eyes fully. He gave her a kiss on the cheek before going up to the counter and ordering himself a drink and a second for Birdie. She was thankful for the gesture and trusted him to order as he knew all of her favorite drinks by now.

She finally pulled out her journal when he came back and sat down, across from her this time so as to give her space to open up to the pages about all of her thoughts and feelings. The entry felt repetitive, echoing the words of the previous entries: love and happiness and butterflies and joy and positivity, all synonyms to her but it still felt important to write it all down.

When they left the cafe, Birdie was finally able to convince Leon to go home and get some rest, and he said he would, but only if she joined him. Another woman would find him clingy, she supposed, but she was enamored and usually happy to follow along. To be honest, she was starting to feel more comfortable in his tiny little apartment than in her overcrowded hostel.

On this specific afternoon though, she insisted that she had to go home, as it had been a while since she'd seen her friends. He pouted for a moment, but of course, respected her decision. They kissed briefly in the street, long past the fear of PDA, and she promised to see him at work the next day.

Walking away from him had become hard for her as their time together went on, and she wondered if she herself wasn't the clingy one. In reality, they both were, which actually made them perfect for one another, though slightly annoying to the general public. She thought of him her whole walk home, but this was not unusual, as he had been the main character in many of her thoughts for some time.

When she arrived home, she was surprised to hear unfamiliar laughter coming from the living space and a few new pairs of shoes by the door. She made her way to the sound of the laughter and was greeted with smiling faces, one of them new. She smiled back at everyone, laughing in embarrassment when Emma made a joke about how long she had been gone. When everyone went back to the conversation, Birdie made her way over to the new girl and introduced herself.

"I'm Naomi," said the new face, "it's great to meet you!" Her features showed such genuineness, and Birdie couldn't help but to be completely drawn in. They talked for hours, exchanging stories and compliments. Birdie could feel, right off the bat, that they would become fast friends. She couldn't explain it, but something clicked between the two of them in a way she had not yet clicked with anyone here, save Leon.

They continued talking long after everyone else had gone to sleep, both glad to be getting to know one another. It seemed to Birdie that Naomi was equally excited about their friendship, and she was looking forward to seeing where it would go. Birdie texted a very sleepy Leon about the encounter throughout, and his excitement was clear through the screen; he knew she had made friends with Emma and Bre, but this seemed more special and he was happy for his girlfriend.

After hours of get-to-knows, they made plans for the following afternoon, and finally went to sleep, both thoroughly tired. Birdie smiled to herself as she dozed off, thankful to have made a friend, and excited for the stories that it would bring into her life.

***

The librarian had stopped drinking his latte long ago, and it sat forgotten on the sill of the window. He had taken occasional breaks as he read and he spent them just staring, taking in the dawn and thinking. I was surprised, actually, that he had stuck with her story for this long. Of course, I wanted him to, but I had forgotten how simple this section was. I thought he would bore himself again, but the fact that he hadn't was wonderful news to me. And as much as I was still concerned, I took a moment to feel grateful for his experience... Maybe he was starting to feel almost human too.

I wished, once again, that we could have a conversation about what he was thinking, hopefully something to ease my concern, but he stayed silent. Frankly, that only escalated my worry. I tried to chalk it up to simple anxiety, but I'd never felt that with his reading before; I'd never seen these expressions. All I could do at this point was hope for the best—hope I didn't make a mistake—, so that's what I did.

***

Naomi followed excitedly behind Birdie as they headed to her favorite cafe, looking forward to meeting Leon after hearing so much about him. He smiled brightly as they entered, and quickly ran around from behind the counter to pull Birdie into a tight embrace. She smiled as Leon leaned in to kiss her, and giggled a little when he remembered where he was and instead opted to hold her tighter. She was thankful that the cafe was near empty, never wanting him to get into trouble on her account.

Leon was enthusiastic when he met Naomi, having never met one of his girlfriend's friends before, aside from speaking over the phone with Emma. Birdie blushed at his excitement, feeling exceptionally lucky to have someone so interested in her and eager to be integrated into her life. Naomi seemed equally happy to meet him, smiling the way she had when she connected with Birdie.

The two girls sat in Birdie's usual spot, sinking into the armchairs with their respective drinks. Birdie had opted out of bringing her journal for the day, wanting to take the opportunity to mindfully get to know Naomi. They sat and spoke as the hours passed, never running out of conversational material. They talked about favorite things, majors in school, reasons for travel, and anything they could think of. Birdie poured her heart out, feeling safe and understood around her new friend. Naomi, she thought, was doing the same.

Birdie, feeling completely open, told Naomi things about herself that she had only confided to her therapist, her journal, and Leon up until this point; she talked about her mental health struggles and family issues, and everything else that led her up to this point in her life. She talked about how she had initially felt that she had come to London as an escape, a way to run away from her life, but in her time there she had discovered that she was finding her true path. Naomi listened intently, soaking in every word, but didn't give much in response. She seemed to know that she was easy to talk to.

Birdie gave a big hug to Leon before leaving the cafe, and she and Naomi walked along the Thames for about an hour before going back home. Birdie started trying to explain things about the city, but Naomi quickly cut her off, explaining that she had actually been there a few times before, and was just coming back to visit for a while. She started trying to explain things to Birdie instead, leaving Birdie with an uncomfortable feeling in her gut, but she was too quiet and polite to butt in. She listened to facts she already knew as if it was the first time, not wanting to make her new friend feel shut down and not thinking about the double standard.

Birdie said a brief goodbye as she dropped Naomi by the hostel, feeling that, though she thoroughly enjoyed being with her, she needed some time alone. She felt an odd longing to journal, realizing that this day may have been the first in a while where she had neglected it. She grabbed her bag of stationery and her journal and made her way back to the cafe.

When Birdie arrived, she saw that Leon was hanging up his apron; his shift must have ended early, and she was surprised that he hadn't told her. He looked at her in shock when he turned around before a huge smile spread across his face and he ran to scoop her up in his arms.

"I was gonna surprise you," he whispered in her ear, "Let's go to dinner?" Birdie laughed, happy at the invitation, thoughts of her much-needed journaling escaping even the back of her mind. She quickly agreed, and they started walking aimlessly together, undecided yet on where to go.

They eventually decided on an all-day breakfast restaurant with the ambiance of a classic diner; Leon said he had been craving pancakes all day, and Birdie was more than happy with that. They shared a huge stack of flapjacks with blueberries, raspberries, and cream, savoring every bite. Leon took a fingerful of cream and put it on Birdie's unsuspecting nose. Her eyes widened and she looked at him with playful annoyance before trying to lick it away, and Leon laughed at the attempt. She wiped it away with a napkin before he leaned in to finally kiss her for the first time that day.

She went home with him, which neither had planned, but both were more than happy about. Their life was beginning to feel very domestic, but not boring, not repetitive, just comfortable and connected. They always smiled into their kisses and made love like it was their first time, butterflies running through both of them all the way. Birdie was always happy to wake up in his arms, and he was always happy to hold her there. They were the perfect match.

The following morning Birdie woke before her boyfriend and went to make herself a coffee, now comfortable with the espresso machine after he taught her how to use it. She sat on the small loveseat in his living area, finally pulling out her stationery and journal. She decorated the pages she planned to write in with greens and pinks—her favorite color combination—and set herself up to begin writing.

Her thoughts flowed with her pen, and she started off by writing about her meeting with Naomi and how immediately she felt they connected. She was surprised, though, when her words transformed from bright and positive, matching the stationery, to apprehensive and anxious. She didn't realize she had felt this way yesterday, or maybe she had and had just suppressed it; she was very good at doing that. Maybe something was off about Naomi... Or maybe she was just holding herself back from a new connection, afraid to mess up the happiness she had discovered in her time there. She wasn't certain.

She supposed that this is why she journaled, she discovered something she didn't yet know about herself or her feelings often, but never to this extent. It felt so drastic, in fact, that she figured she must have been dramatizing for some reason, and she quickly followed her ominous paragraphs with words on her amazing night with Leon.

He woke shortly after she finished writing, just as she was climbing back under the covers to join him again. She didn't notice his eyes open and started a little when he hugged her to him, causing him to laugh. They hadn't said it yet, but to anyone looking in on their relationship, it was clear that they were in love. The way that they looked at one another, there was no other explanation.

***

At this point, I saw a sure look of disdain pass over the librarian's face, and it solidified my building suspicions and anxieties. Something was very wrong, and at this moment, I didn't hope, but prayed, that it wasn't what my intuition led me to believe.

It seemed I had given this special piece of literature to a selfish being, an ill-fit colleague. I tried to justify to myself, how could I have known? He hardly opened up to me, but I felt that I should have known better, and after all this time, I thought I did. It seemed he was still a mystery to me, an enigma with all the wrong priorities. I felt so stupid, and he stayed so silent, just looking angrily at the page in front of him. He wasn't empathetic, he was selfish, all of my hopes immediately dashed just with that one look on his face.

He looked up from the book for a moment and opened his mouth to say something while I listened intently, but he closed it just as fast. I watched in suspense until he did something that shouldn't have surprised me after all the thoughts that had just rushed through my head. He started flipping through the book, skimming the following pages like they didn't matter, like they weren't an equally important part of her story, like everything else he had read.

He flipped through at least a month, before finally landing on a random page. I knew what he was hoping for, as much as I wanted to deny it, and I knew he wouldn't find it there, but I held my tongue, praying that he'd continue reading and his mind would clear up or change.

I didn't give him anything, I didn't care what he wanted. He could get it himself. But he stayed firmly planted in his seat and continued reading.

***

Birdie cursed herself for being so quick to trust as she tore her room apart, searching endlessly for her precious journal. Tears had long past welled up in her eyes and were now pouring down her face, dripping from her chin down onto her shirt. Naomi hadn't been gone long at all before Birdie realized it was missing, and she was certain that Naomi was the reason for its disappearance, but she searched and searched nonetheless.

The other girls tried to mind their own business, but Emma did what she could to help Birdie search. She recognized and understood how important the journal was to her, and wanted her to find it. This was a horrible way to feel.

While they looked, Bre listened intently to Cecilia and Leeh, Naomi's prior roommates, who knew the whole story of her disappearance and were filling in the other girls.

It had only been about two hours since Naomi was asked to leave by their host, something the lovely old lady had never had to do before; she was extremely non confrontational, and could never have even imagined a situation like this one.

Birdie heard the girls shriek in the other room and came running, only to find them throwing a condom wrapper to one another like it was a hot potato. In between shrieks and her own sobs, she was able to decipher that it had fallen down onto Leeh's bed from the bunk above, where Naomi used to sleep.

To put it simply, Naomi had crossed countless boundaries with the other girls in the hostel, especially those she shared a room with. Having her boy toy come over in the dead of night, surprising the girls when they woke to see him asleep in Naomi's bed, was the last straw. The host was quick to kick her out, giving no warning and no second chance; she didn't deserve them. No one, except Birdie, was shocked at all.

Birdie had spoken to Naomi right after she heard the news, wanting to be there, a shoulder to cry on for her friend. But her friend didn't cry, she just stared ahead, eyes void of any emotion. Birdie was concerned for Naomi and angry at the girls for reporting her without asking her first to make a change, but there was a lot she didn't know.

Naomi gaslit Birdie, telling her a vast array of lies, saying that the girls knew that the unknown man was coming over and were okay with it, on top of further lies and exaggerations about how her roommates had treated her.

If that were true, Birdie would have had every right to be angry at the girls for reporting, but they had shown her, before she went looking for her journal, text receipts that proved that Naomi treated them rudely and had never once asked the girls permission for his presence.

Birdie knew none of this, and of course, felt awful upon the discoveries for jumping to conclusions and trusting Naomi before any of the girls she had been living with for so long. Birdie felt completely betrayed and manipulated; she had fallen for every word Naomi had said just because they "clicked". And now that Naomi was gone, her journal, her most personal possession, had gone missing. She ran back into her room and broke down crying and Emma ran in to comfort her as best she could.

This was a nightmare. She had spent so long working on her mental stability and clarity and it felt like it was all going to crumble in a single second, like all of her efforts were for nothing. Emma took Birdie's phone and dialed Leon, who she had now met on a few occasions, and asked him to come over quickly. Thankfully, he wasn't working that day, in fact, he had been preparing himself to call Birdie any second, and he was out the door before even hanging up.

By the time he arrived, Birdie had taken a pill for her anxiety and she felt she was beginning to calm down. She was no longer heaving for breath, but tears still streamed down her face. The girls let him into the hostel, significantly more comfortable with him than with Naomi's mystery boy. He scooped Birdie into his arms the moment he saw her, and she tried to hold in her pain, not wanting him to see her in the state she was in, but she wasn't able to.

In a few words, she was able to express to Leon that she needed to be away from the crowdedness of the hostel as soon as possible, and he made quick work of ordering them a cab, not wanting her to have to walk all the way to his as upset as she was. She looked at him with gratitude, though her eyes were still clouded with tears.

H er tears had finally dried as she laid curled up under his blankets. He laid next to her but on top of the blankets, wanting to give her the space to privately recover, not wanting her to feel as if he was suffocating her. She was thankful for his thoughtfulness and also his presence.

She eventually rolled over to face him again and let him caress her cheek, even giving a weak smile when he did so. He made her dinner and cared for her as the tear stains dissipated from her face and her color started to return.

This day had been exceptionally distressing and she just couldn't imagine it getting worse, but she thought too soon. Leon came running back towards her as Birdie stared at her phone in disbelief, jaw slack and tears welling up once again. He glanced at the screen and saw pages and pages with sticker-decorated corners, clearly ripped out of a journal. He realized what it was immediately and didn't read a word, instead looking back to Birdie and cupping her face in his hands.

Birdie was in disbelief. Naomi had not only taken her journal but had posted the most intimate and personal pages to her public social media pages, tagging her. Birdie had no idea of what she could have done to bother or upset Naomi, and she certainly didn't deserve this.

Soon, her phone was flooded with texts from her friends and roommates, some checking in on her, and some cluelessly asking if a vague journal entry was about them. She was absolutely convinced that Leon was the only one who wouldn't read them and she pulled herself closer to his chest. He felt the movement and held her tightly; he would never let go if that's what she needed, and for the time being that's how she felt.

***

The librarian looked up and allowed the book to fall from his hands. This was not what he wanted and certainly not what he expected. I watched the look of disbelief and betrayal on his face, though he couldn't blame me this time; he had chosen this volume for himself.

"That bitch," the librarian finally spoke, after these past hours of silence, and for once I agreed. I felt that way even as I wrote Naomi's story, and I remembered questioning the purpose of such cruelty. But, I supposed, some people are just cruel for the sake of it. "I just- I can't believe she would, or even could, do that," he continued. I watched him silently as he once again closed his mouth, staring at the book on the floor.

We sat like that in silence for a long time, his eyes never leaving that silver moon on the cover. Finally, he weakly kicked it, and it slid just far enough to go straight under the shelf he had pulled it from. No longer dawdling, he followed it and searched through the volumes, once again trying to intuitively pick the *right* one.

When he finally pulled his chosen book from its place on the shelf, I kept silent and made no move to correct him. I, of course, knew the volume, but I didn't think it was the right time for me to step into his decisions, not with all the anger I knew he was bottling up at that moment.

In retrospect, I wonder if stepping in then would have changed the following half hour, changed the path he chose...

He moved swiftly back to his seat, and I once again made no move to bring him anything; I felt that I needed to watch for the time being. I had to be sure of my suspicions, though I didn't know what I would do if I was proven correct.

He flipped to a page towards the end of the volume and started reading.

***

Naomi followed excitedly behind Birdie as they headed to her favorite cafe, looking forward to meeting Leon after hearing so much about him. He smiled brightly as they entered, and quickly ran around from behind the counter to pull Birdie into a tight embrace. She smiled as Leon leaned in to kiss her, and giggled a little when he remembered where he was and instead opted to hold her tighter. She was thankful that the cafe was near empty, never wanting him to get into trouble on her account.

Leon was enthusiastic when he met Naomi, having never met one of his girlfriend's friends before, aside from speaking over the phone with Emma. Birdie blushed at his excitement, feeling exceptionally lucky to have someone so interested in her and eager to be integrated into her life. Naomi seemed equally happy to meet him, as she herself was thankful to be brought into Birdie's life so quickly. Birdie didn't think this at the time, but Naomi seemed a little too excited to meet Leon. She also didn't notice the way Leon's eyes began to track her friend instead of herself as the two of them talked over their drinks.

Their time at the cafe was brief, and Birdie started to feel a strange sense of discomfort as she talked with her new friend. Something was just... off. She tried to suppress the thought, chalking it up to anxiety about letting someone into her life the way she was. She had worn her heart on her sleeve as they talked, allowing Naomi in on many secrets she had only yet shared with her therapist, journal, and Leon, each confession being quickly followed by a sense of regret, but it seemed she couldn't stop; Naomi was just too easy to talk to.

Her discomfort only grew as they walked together along the river, Naomi condescendingly sharing facts about a city Birdie had been in for well over two months now, never letting her get a word in. She was feeling more and more regretful as the time went on, and she decided at that moment to take a step back from Naomi as friends; maybe they were just meant to be acquaintances. She, again, regretted all the personal things she had spilled to her in confidence, as she felt that confidence dissolving.

B irdie stood in shock outside the club; nothing could have prepared her for Naomi's emotional outburst and anger. The boy she had brought with her—Birdie couldn't bring herself to remember his name—had kissed another girl, not thinking that he and Naomi were out *together*; he thought the outing was much more casual than she did. Naomi screamed at Birdie as if it was her fault, and, though she wasn't directly blaming her, she was overwhelmed with anger and only directing it at Birdie because she was there. Birdie, however, had decided days ago, when she had first met Naomi and started to feel a sense of discomfort around her, that she wasn't going to take any pain for this girl.

The shock soon disappeared from her face and was replaced with apathy, and she did something she had never before had the guts to do: she just walked away. Naomi followed for a bit, screaming all the way, before huffing and stopping to light a cigarette.

Birdie took a moment to breathe in some fresh air, not wanting to allow Naomi's outburst to bring down her energy any more than it already had. When she finally brought herself back into the club, she found Leon and stated that she wanted to go home. She was tired. He smiled at her, but the warmth his smile usually brought didn't light up inside her and she felt uneasy. Maybe it was just an aftereffect of the altercation outside.

When they left, she was shocked that he didn't start leading her to his apartment, but instead to her hostel. She stayed quiet, after all, a night alone might be what she needed for the time being. She deeply hoped that Naomi and her boy toy would reconcile and that she wouldn't have to face either a dishonest apology or stone-faced, closeted anger.

She kissed Leon goodnight at the door, and he pulled her in for a hug. Maybe she was just drunk, but his embrace didn't feel as tight as usual and she gave him a half smile before walking through the threshold of her home.

Birdie sat in the living space with Emma, drinking tea and detailing to her all the events of the night. She was exhausted, but needed to vent to someone before going to bed, as she didn't want to hold on to all the emotions surrounding the night and she was too tired to journal. Emma, as always, responded with exaggerated facial reactions and words of agreeance, equally as shocked about the events of the night as Birdie had been. They both prayed that Naomi wouldn't walk in through the door as they spoke, though they agreed to continue talking if she did; they were feeling petty and felt she deserved to hear some of the frustrations about her right to her face.

Luckily though, their prayers were answered, and she never arrived home. Birdie went to sleep late at night, or early in the morning, however you want to look at it. She slept heavily, oddly thankful to be in her own bed, but with a heavy weight on her chest as she rested.

B irdie awoke from a dream into a nightmare. Emma shook her to consciousness, a look of urgency and second-hand sadness on her face; Birdie couldn't imagine the cause in her groggy state.

She blinked the sleep from her eyes for a moment before finally looking up at Emma's phone from her low bunk, and they widened at what she saw. She first recognized a photo of Leon making coffee in his apartment, but her heart broke when she saw that it had been posted to Naomi's story. The next slide was of her giving him a kiss, but the camera was angled from behind his head, so Birdie was almost certain that he didn't know that the photo was being taken. Naomi did this to hurt Birdie, to get revenge on her for walking away. Leon did this because he was a coward.

The sleep in Birdie's eyes was soon replaced by tears, and she laid back down to curl up and sob. She couldn't believe this. She had finally fallen in love, for the first time in her life, only for it to end like this. Emma sat at the end of the bed, saying nothing, but Birdie was thankful for her support; just her presence was enough.

Finally, she worked up the courage to call Leon, and his line went almost immediately to voicemail. He texted her that he was having breakfast with a friend, which was half true, as Naomi had just posted another sneaky photo of him from his apartment with some food they had ordered in. Birdie had no words in response. She simply texted him the screenshots of the story and put her phone on silent, finally walking out into the kitchen to make some coffee for herself.

She had moved on, temporarily, from feeling distraught to feeling outraged, and her roommates were more than happy to listen, empathizing with her anger. Cecelia and Leeh called the host, asking for a form to petition the removal of Naomi from the hostel, as there was no direct violation of any of the rules; they were all just sick and tired of her drama and the repercussions that she didn't seem to notice. She could stay on the street, or with Leon, for all Birdie cared.

When she finally picked her phone back up she had a dozen missed calls from her soon to be ex-boyfriend, as well as a string of apologetic texts.

"i kicked her out"

"i'm so sorry"

"please call me"

"i love you"

Birdie scoffed as she read those and more, feeling overrun with anger and disgust. By the time Naomi arrived back home, the host had brought by a form and all the girls had signed it. She had until the end of the day to pack up her things and get out; she was no longer welcome.

It didn't take long, though, for Birdie's feelings to devolve back into sadness and she finally, after hours of commiserating with her roommates, picked up the phone to respond to Leon. His voice was urgent and pleading as he begged Birdie not to leave him, almost crying into his end of the phone. His tears were triggering to her, as she had always sympathized with him so deeply, but she fought hard to hold back the tears that were threatening to fall down her own cheeks. She ended things, right there on that phone call, and hung up, sadness and anger melding together in her heart.

She looked at Naomi with the fire of hate burning behind her irises as she walked her things out of the hostel. Birdie saw a look that verged on apologetic in Naomi's eyes, but she would never accept it. Their friendship was over, ruined, and after only a mere 72 hours. Birdie was too angry at the time to think of it, but she would learn a lot of lessons from this disaster of a friendship and her broken relationship, the main one being not to trust as easily as she always had. But for now, she was broken-hearted and betrayed.

***

I was surprised that the librarian had continued reading this far, I thought that he would have given up paragraphs ago. What should have surprised me too was seeing a thoughtless smile cross his face, but it only confirmed my worries as he read: he had lost the empathy that he had grown for Birdie, and had replaced it with infatuation.

That was a problem. That had never happened before, and I had no idea what repercussions would follow if he didn't snap out of it. I started to panic, and I had no idea what I could do to change his path. It was becoming dangerous for him, for me, for Birdie... For everything.

It was probably too late to change anything, but I had to try. I quickly pulled another volume off of the shelf, one that would hopefully bring him back onto the path of empathy. I prayed that it wasn't too late as I laid it down on the table in front of him. He looked up from the book as I did so, and I saw something that looked like disdain cross his face, for me or for the story, I did not know. Reluctantly, he set down the volume he was holding and picked up the one I had chosen for him. He didn't move to get a refreshment or food, he didn't look out the window, he just opened the pages and started reading.

It isn't even worth it to include an excerpt here, that's how quickly he decided he didn't like it. This volume was a favorite of mine, one in which Naomi never moves into the hostel and Birdie continues her relationship happily with Leon. Granted, it's a little mundane and repetitive, but it's positive for Birdie, a story she deserves and a future she wants.

I was in utter shock as he momentarily looked up from the book, which seemed innocent enough at first, but quickly turned dangerous as his gaze snapped back and he started ripping out pages, starting with the beginning of her relationship with Leon. This path was one of her happiest, and I didn't know if he was aware that he was taking this joy away from her. Her paths, like everyone else's, were ultimately unlimited, but limited to the ink on the various tellings of them, and it was unfair of him to play God and destroy what her life could have been. But that's what he was doing; it was mindless and thoughtless and driven from a place of greed, but he continued. As he tore the pages out, the pages following turned blank, her story being erased.

I watched his face change as he noticed this, and terror filled me as he threw the volume to the side and marched toward the shelf of her story. He started pulling out each volume, tearing out the story of her meeting Leon, once again, in the first. In the second, he tore out the pages starting with her meeting Naomi, and again the pages erased themselves in the back. He continued until the next volume he pulled was blank entirely, having been affected by the destruction he caused already.

I was frozen, horrified as my work was destroyed, but I shook myself out of it; I had to stop him. Not knowing what else to do, I pushed the shelf as hard as I could toward him. He was distracted for a moment, looking at the empty volume, but he yelled and lept out of the way as the towering shelf toppled in his direction. He watched angrily as it took down the shelf next to it, and the one after that, scattering books from hundreds of paths in dozens of stories onto the ground. He was angry with me, probably because he thought he'd have to clean this up, but I saw his face change, like he had come to the resolve of no longer doing his job, no longer carrying out his purpose.

"Fuck you!" he yelled, words he had never directed towards me in all our time together, "You could have seriously hurt me!" I didn't care, I was furious. It's not like he would have felt anything real anyway.

He had become destructive and was destroying everything I had created, everything he was meant to protect and upkeep and I was at a loss for how to fix it. He and I were the only ones here, and to the extent of my almost endless knowledge, there were no replacements. We were done for.

Though he was furious with me, as I was with him, the falling shelves seemed to have knocked some sense, if not fear, into him. He dragged his feet as he walked back towards the book he had last been reading, the volume of devastation that he had left untouched in his destruction of so many of her joys.

He sat back down on that little seat by the window, and something caught his eye as it did mine. We looked outside the window and, instead of the beautiful moments before the sunrise, dusk had fallen. Stars were beginning to appear in the sky as the sun settled further and further beyond the horizon, a sight neither he nor I were familiar with. This seemed to further his resolve; he had convinced himself he was in the right, and this sudden shift in the beautiful sky was only proof of this to me. It seemed his desperation for change had overtaken him and that he had accepted all change as a triumph on his part, even one in the sky. I felt, in that moment, I read his features better than I ever had: He was delusional.

He flipped the book open, a few pages beyond where he had left off.

***

Tears streamed freely from Birdie's eyes as the cab made its way to her BnB, though she was embarrassed. The usually chatty driver had caught one glimpse of her face and decided it was for the best to leave her to her thoughts. She was devastated. Emma, of all people, was the last one she would expect to walk in on reading her journal. Whatever the purpose was, Birdie simply couldn't grasp it, regardless of how many excuses she gave.

"I just loved the stationery!"

"You weren't telling me enough about how Leon made you feel, I wanted to understand!"

"Well, you told Naomi this stuff!"

None of those excuses even partially made up for the damage done. Birdie had no idea how much Emma had read once she walked into the room, no idea how much of her poured out soul had been exposed.

Birdie never could have expected it, but Emma switched up from the defense to the offense shockingly quickly, accusing Birdie, stating that some of the journal entries were about her. And to be fair, they were, though not all the ones she was referencing in her anger. Birdie was furious, it's not like she was going to try to publish, it was her *diary*. It was none of Emma's business what she wrote, regardless of whether it was about her or not.

This experience caused her to realize the lack of boundaries in their relationship. Emma was always way too upfront with very personal questions, whether they were about mental health or sex or anything else, it didn't matter; it was exhausting and Birdie hadn't really allowed herself to accept it. She was just happy to be living with such a close friend.

Birdie's thoughts were cut off as her cab pulled up in front of a small but cute apartment building which housed the BnB and the driver helped her carry her bags to the door. She thanked him timidly before struggling with the front door code, feeling overwhelmed with relief when she figured it out and got inside. The idea of being seen by anyone at that moment, even the driver, was exhausting. She dragged her two bags up the stairs, as there was no elevator, and finally let herself into her room.

It was cute, and the bed was much larger than the one she had in her hostel, which she was exceptionally thankful for. She plopped down onto it, allowing the squishy mattress to pull her into its embrace. She decided to unpack later as she wrapped herself up in the blankets, allowing the tears to fall again, wanting nothing more than to be welcomed by sleep.

S leep did eventually overtake her, and she woke up with puffy and crusty eyes. Birdie felt as though she had lost everything in under a week, and she just didn't understand how it could all go downhill so quickly. She missed Leon more than anything. She thought to journal, but the second she pulled it out and looked at it, she felt this overwhelming shock of trauma, and realized that her friendship-ending interaction with Emma had messed her up more than she originally thought.

Too many distressing things had happened to her in the past week. Birdie was exceptionally frustrated, sad, and angry. She didn't know what to do with all of those emotions, so she just balled herself up in her bed and cried. She tried not to beat herself up for having that reaction, but her time in London was running out bit by bit every day and she didn't want to waste it. Nonetheless, she didn't know how she was going to get out into the world in her current state. She thought to call her mother, who was always such a guiding light when she was distraught, but she didn't pick up the phone, so Birdie just continued to cry.

***

The librarian skimmed through the next few pages and found that they were repetitive and depressing, just a loop of Birdie crying and wasting her time wrapped in the blankets of her BnB. He stopped skimming and just started flipping pages, and I saw his face turn white as he reached the point towards the end where the pages, just like the ones in the other volumes, eventually turned blank. I saw panic in his eyes, and thought that maybe he regretted destroying so many of her futures. He flipped back to the last written page.

***

Birdie stood on the bridge, crying for the last time. She said a silent thank you to the positive experiences she'd had, and an equally silent wish that there had been more. She thought of Leon, Naomi, Emma, her family, all of the people that had wronged her in the past weeks, and she wished that she were stronger—

***

He slammed the book closed, and for the first time I saw the terror that should have been there the whole time as he destroyed my—no, *her*—stories. He had left her there, in her worst possible path, and there was nothing he could do to fix it after the destruction he had left in pursuit of his personal gain. I didn't know if that was remorse on his face or simply shock, or maybe, terrifyingly, it was budding satisfaction. 'If I can't have you no one can' and all that.

I wasn't surprised when he ripped out those last few pages, leaving Birdie crying in her BnB. What did surprise me, though, is that he summoned a pen and stared at the empty pages before him.

I was terrified. I had no idea what would happen. He was going to try to write her story, to change the outcome, all to satisfy his jealous need for a 'proper' ending. This was catastrophic. That was my job and he had no right to infringe upon it, and I had no idea what would happen to me if he tried. But he didn't care. He was angry with me and desperate to satisfy his own desire for closure. It was selfish, thoughtless, and awful. I was completely at a loss.

I felt a sharp pain as he brought pen to paper. I knocked over another shelf and a domino effect ensued around him, but he paid no mind, he just kept writing. This was the end of me, I thought, and I prayed that something would come over him to make him stop, but I knew my prayers were in vain.

After days of sorrow, Birdie finally worked up the energy to leave her BnB and go somewhere other than the convenience store for a meal. That was where she met him: Thomas. He looked studious and thoughtful, sitting in the corner of the cafe, drinking his tea and eating a small tiramisu. He seemed to sense her presence as she entered, and looked up through his glasses to see her. He was taken aback by her beauty, and he knew he had to make her his.

***

I watched in horror as Thomas, as he had named himself, dissolved into the air, phasing away from his seat, as the words began to write themselves. I never could have expected this, and I think he was surprised as well. He disappeared into the pages and I could sense that the story was taking place now through his thoughts alone, like a lucid dream. He was going to destroy her story, and, for all I knew, take all the other ones down with him. He was reckless and I began to hate him, a feeling I was not familiar with.

***

Once she ordered, something compelled Birdie to take the seat next to him, boldly introducing herself. He smiled and began to speak to her, and she didn't know, but this was his first time having a conversation with anyone other than his previous colleague. He was surprisingly charismatic, and they got along well immediately. He made her smile in ways she hadn't since she parted with Leon, and she didn't know how to feel. For some reason, she felt like a traitor, though she was the one who had been betrayed.

What she couldn't explain was the way he spoke. His words almost didn't register in her mind; she could comprehend the meaning but not the phonetic sounds that he was making. No one else seemed to notice, so she chalked it up to the heaviness of his Irish accent. She must have been imagining things.

Thomas asked her to accompany him on a walk, and they found themselves strolling alongside the Thames, Birdie's favorite place. Thomas stationed himself between the guardrail and Birdie throughout, reminding himself of the end for her that he had prevented and hoping that nothing would lead her to that anymore. She seemed happy on this day, and he would do anything to keep it that way.

He walked her to her BnB, and boldly kissed her as he said goodbye. He felt something nearing guilt, realizing she would like it no matter what—he had written it so—but that feeling was inconsequential compared to the happiness he felt being in her presence. Birdie went inside, butterflies in her stomach and joy in her heart.

She felt slightly taken aback as she walked through the threshold of the BnB, as the butterflies she felt inside her materialized in the corner of her eye, but she was unable to look at them directly. The blues and oranges and purples flitted in the edges of her vision like a mirage, but she knew they were there, dancing in the receding sunlight.

She sat in her room and finally summoned the courage to pull out her journal, jotting down happy feelings for the first time in the week since she had left Leon. She was embarrassed to be moving on so quickly, Leon had been her first love after all, but she justified this by reminding herself that rebounds could be healthy if done correctly. As Thomas planned, this was meant to be a positive experience for both of them.

Birdie saw a light in the corner of her eye and looked up quickly, only to be utterly shocked by what she witnessed. There, in front of her, was a fairy with glowing wings, flying through the air. It vaguely resembled the fairies she had seen in her childhood cartoons, with a cute short dress and dragonfly wings, a small bun in her hair. She was soon joined by more, quickly becoming a legion as they lit up her room like fireflies. They danced around her, twinkling like stars, filling her with awe.

***

Thomas phased back into his seat, a look of confusion plastered across his face. I looked at the work on the pages in Birdie's—no, now Thomas's—story, and saw that they were merging and shifting. His story was changing, no longer following what he had written.

I was right; he had destroyed everything I had worked so hard to build. Her world was crumbling and I was sure that others would soon too. But Thomas was not affected, he continued writing, periodically appearing and disappearing from our reality.

***

When Birdie awoke, the fairies that had danced around her all throughout the night were gone, where, she didn't know. They had left her with a sense of awe, a new curiosity for the secrets of the world piqued inside her. She looked outside and saw an almost orange sky, and, though it was daylight, she could have sworn she saw a second moon, shining bright and seeming closer to the world than it should have been.

She moved outside, admiring the amber sky and looking around for Thomas, who said he would pick her up at ten A.M. She looked forward to her date, happy to be getting her mind off all of the pains she had felt in the past week and excited to create new stories and admire the unexpected changes she was witnessing in the world. When he arrived she smiled at him and he returned the gesture, with no necessary exchange of words.

They, once again, walked to the river—which now shimmered almost silver instead of its usual murky brown—, Thomas always standing between Birdie and the guardrail. He was on edge, confused about how things had been so out of his control, and feeling a deep-down terror that Birdie might revert to her original story, jumping into the shimmery current. He wouldn't allow it.

They had a beautiful day, stopping briefly for a meal and ice cream, sitting together in a bright and beautiful park and exchanging stories. Birdie, of course, didn't know this, but Thomas's stories were partially fabricated and partially stolen from the millennia of reading he had experienced. He did his best not to let on everything he knew about her life and past, but whenever he let something slip he made sure she just believed it was intuition on his part.

A few hours into their date, the sky darkened to a gray of an unusual shade and rain began to fall.

This was not surprising for London, but the day soon took a turn for the worse when they heard a terrifying roar come from the clouds. Birdie looked up to see a horrid beast swoop down into their atmosphere, its red eyes glowing in the distance. She felt an immense fear, accompanied by an odd feeling of deja vu. The cloud-like texture of what looked like fur was undeniably familiar, and she racked her brain for where she may have seen it before through her terror.

Thomas took her hand and they began running, trying to quickly get into a denser area and out of danger. The beast swept down, gliding along the top of the Thames before it crashed into a tourist ferry. As it hit the water, it dissolved, like a cloud condensing into the river itself, leaving nothing in its wake but a destroyed boat and some devastating casualties.

Thomas and Birdie walked briskly, almost jogging back to her BnB, where he gave her a warm hug and a long kiss goodbye, wanting to savor each moment with her before he lost control of the world he had corrupted. She held onto him tightly, but was eager to get back inside, afraid of what else might materialize itself from the clouds.

***

Thomas phased back into the library and pulled the pen away from the pages of Birdie's story, suddenly afraid and desperate to avoid any further damage. But it was too late, he was too far gone and so was her future.

In his absence, I had flipped through a plethora of stories and discovered that their words were merging and shifting, new stories being created or changed and some stories erasing themselves completely. As I suspected, Thomas had, in a selfish and irrational instinct, destroyed everything I had created—the universe and all its possibilities as it was meant to be.

Everything was falling into chaos, and I think he was finally beginning to wrap his mind around that. I chose not to alert him of the changes he had yet to notice in Birdie's story during his absence.

The end was coming. My characters would call it judgment, the apocalypse, whatever suited their fancy, if they even had the willpower or autonomy to do so.

I took it upon myself to throw a volume at him, and he jumped as it whizzed right past his head. A perfect distraction. He practically ran to pick it up, to see what there was I needed him to see. I felt no sympathy as he opened the pages and saw the destruction he had caused.

***

But Alexander took the next step anyway, silently drawing an arrow from his waist and taking aim. His father sat silently, terrified, staring down the tip of the arrow, too sad to look his son in the eyes. He had no idea what could have brought his boy to this, what he had done or hadn't done to cause it to end this way. But he saw no remorse in the boy's eyes, and a tear fell as he took his final breath.

***

As he read, I watched Birdie's story contort and shift, time passing in an unusually quick fashion. Two of her days later, I felt horror as her realities clashed, an explosion of paradox.

***

Birdie could have sworn she was looking in a mirror. Standing in front of her was a replica of herself with the same look of confusion and alarm on her identical face. They stood in silence for a moment before the copy spoke.

"Who are—?I—? How are you me?"

"I don't know..." Birdie answered timidly, her anxieties closing in on her in an instant. She had become oddly accustomed to the creatures and chaos surrounding her, but this was the final straw.

"Seriously, who are you?" said the other Birdie, sounding almost aggressive in tone. It was clear to Birdie from this interaction alone that the clone, or whatever she was, carried herself with greater confidence than Birdie herself, or at least presented a flawless facade of doing so.

"I don't know..." Birdie reiterated, irritating the mirror image before her. Unsure of how to feel or communicate, Birdie ran out the door of the cafe and into the chaotic city of London under its orange sky. She rested for a moment, catching her breath, eyes training upwards. She couldn't begin to understand how she had so easily accepted all the changes around her; it felt as though she had had an epiphany through thoughts that were not her own.

Out of blind instinct, Birdie ran back inside, startling her duplicate.

"What color is the sky?" Birdie asked, sounding almost delirious, eyes wide with realization.

"Are you blind? It's orange, just like it's always been."

Birdie felt tears well up in her eyes. How had she woken up mere days ago to wonder and terror, just accepting it? How did she arrive in this strange reality with two moons and a silver river, and how could she already be there for herself to meet? The possibilities suddenly felt endless, and her head throbbed. She thought things like this only happened in books...

***

I was horrified. This was never meant to happen, and I couldn't even begin to imagine what her human brain must be experiencing as it exploded with new revelations. She didn't deserve this pain and I felt that I had failed in my position as caretaker. I knew what had to be done now.

I turned my attention back to Thomas, now afraid and confused, as he threw Alexander's narrative from his hands. It was one he had become vaguely familiar with and seeing such a different outcome struck fear in him.

He looked back down at Birdie's story, a book which he was now co-author to, and saw that the words were still appearing and shifting without his pen, being driven by his inner thoughts, but quickly morphing from them into something else.

I could see the internal dissonance he was experiencing as he wiped the sweat from his brow: should he stay away to avoid further damage, or should he go back and try to save her? I think we both knew at this point that it was far too late for either. He took the leap anyway, and I saw him disappear from between my shelves once again, too preoccupied to notice the rising temperature.

***

Thomas felt confused and disoriented as he appeared, unsure of why he had landed in a park by the Thames of all places. He looked around desperately, searching for any signs of Birdie, of anyone at all, but the landscape was motionless, save for the distant flickering flames of the burning buildings on the other side of the river. He heard far-off yelling and screaming and he momentarily mourned the serenity he had so carelessly destroyed.

That moment ended quickly, though, when he saw a familiar body lying in the grass, struggling to draw breath mere meters from him. He wondered how he had overlooked it, but allowed that thought to drift away as he bolted in her direction, silently praying that it was not who he thought. A flicker of movement caught his eye and he snapped his head towards it only to see the short stature of a creature that looked almost human, its sharp, fingerlike claws glistening red as it lumbered away from the figure.

His prayers, of course, were pointless, and he wailed into the chaos as he held a dying Birdie in his arms, begging for a miracle. Blood flowed steadily from the stab wounds in her abdomen and he wondered what her thoughts had been as she was attacked. Had she cried out for him, wishing for his aid? What a selfish thought.

"Birdie, can you hear me? Stay with me," he cried, shaking her as her consciousness faded. He didn't understand the way she looked at him, first confusion which was quickly covered with disdain.

"Please say something," he begged after a heaving sob.

"I can't understand you..." Birdie whispered, hardly audible as she used the rest of her breath to communicate. Thomas' eyes widened, realization hitting him that the meanings of his words no longer translated in her brain; he had lost complete control of the realities around him.

"Did—did you do this?" Birdie asked, and Thomas tried to speak again before she continued, "Nod for yes." He took a deep breath and allowed his tears to overtake him as he reluctantly nodded, admitting his guilt to the one he loved most.

Birdie looked at him, her expression losing all emotion and turning instead to stone. She never broke eye contact as she uttered her last words:

"Get the fuck away from me."

Her tone expressed her disgust when her face could not. With all the strength left in her dying muscles, she pushed herself away and out of Thomas' arms. He wanted more than anything to hold on, but reality was beginning to set in and he chose to respect Birdie's final wish. His grip loosened and she rolled out of his lap onto the grass. Silent tears rolled out of his eyes as he watched her, he didn't know for how long, but she didn't move again.

Thomas allowed tears to fall harder and louder the longer he watched. He stayed by her side until her skin was white and her veins ran dry, crying out an exhausting repetition of apologies between his sobs. He begged for forgiveness and maybe a second chance, both of which he would never get, nor did he deserve.

***

I felt no pity when Thomas returned to my shelves for the final time, his once nice clothes now covered in Birdie's blood, head in his hands, sobbing. He whimpered out apologies still, never silencing in juxtaposition to the rest of his time here, but I would never accept them. In fact, I didn't know if he was apologizing to me, or to Birdie, and I suppose I never would. I had already lit the fire.

He didn't seem surprised when he looked up and saw the shelves surrounding him ablaze. Maybe he agreed with me; this was the best, no, the *only* option. He had destroyed everything, the universe I had worked so hard to create; all of my characters now cursed to live lives of cruelty and confusion before they are cut short, never to feel love or joy or safety, never to reach the back cover. That was no life.

I thought he might see it as a selfish act, but he seemed to understand. Thomas was, of course, the only one to really be affected by the flames. All of my characters would simply be wiped from existence. I, myself, wasn't sure of what would happen to me, but with no more stories to uphold or write, I assumed I would simply burn to the ground, my shelves and stories left as ash for the wind to blow away. On second thought, I didn't even know if the wind would remain, or that beautiful sunrise turned to dusk; perhaps it would all disappear. If he survived the fire, though, I wondered if Thomas would live on, alone in that emptiness, or if the flames would take him away as well, ending all that would be left of my universe.

"I'm sorry," he pleaded one last time, which I again would not accept. He looked around, desperate to find my face or a pair of eyes, both of which we knew he never would. All he could do was run a gentle but desperate hand down the beams of my shelves, begging for forgiveness and the possibility that I would feel his sincerity. In a final act of disregard, I used the last of my force to drop a flaming book onto his hand, causing him to recoil, never to touch me again. Good riddance.

He seemed, at least, to understand what he had done. He recognized this as his fault, and was going to use his last breaths trying to repent. I don't know what he—who is meant to be steward to every life and every story—believed in, but he seemed to pray, before opening his eyes and walking steadily into the dense flames. I thought I would hear him scream as they engulfed him, but only silence followed in his wake, something so familiar from him that it only made sense that it would follow him to his end. I wished him an equally silent farewell.

On the other hand, I wished I could scream out. I didn't know, couldn't have thought, that the burning would feel so excruciating, but it was a pain I had never even imagined. I tried to find solace, though, in the stories of my beloved characters who now burned as well. The poor civilians across the Thames from Birdie, trapped in those buildings ablaze; I tried to sympathize with them, to take their pain. They didn't deserve any of this, they didn't deserve their painful ends. I hoped it would be over quickly, for their sake and mine.

It feels ironic for me to have written a story for Thomas and the end of all of my created universes, but here it is, my final work. I wonder, as I whisper these words, if it will survive the flames, or if it will be consumed as the rest of my stories have been.

I feel emptiness as this concludes; I wonder whether this will serve as a testament and warning, or if this will cause all stories, as well as mine, to repeat perpetually. My hope is for the former. I hope that, if a new multiverse forms to replace mine, if a new library forms to replace me, that this final work will find its way into the shelves, to serve as a warning against Thomas' mistakes. I hope that any lives written in the future are allowed to experience their timelines as they were written and not as they were destroyed. Mine deserved better than they received.

I feel my final thoughts approaching as the flames die down, and I can't help but feel thankful for all the beautiful stories I was allowed to create and the characters I was able to love so deeply and dearly, though they are gone now. I feel sad, but content at having ending their pain, and thus, I am at peace.

I wonder if my consciousness will continue on, or if it will die out in the embers... I suppose I may never know.

Thank you for allowing me to hold the universe.

I feel nervous. I feel my ... empire approaching as I lie down, and I can't help but feel thankful for all the beautiful stories I was allowed to create and the characters I have ... to love so deeply and dearly, though they're all gone now. I feel sad, but content, at ...

I wonder if my conscience that will carry out ... it will die out the entire ... long time I may ...

Thank you for allowing me to hold the power.